GREENHOUSES & GARDEN SHEDS

Inspiration, Information & Step-by-Step Projects

PAT PRICE *with*
NORA RICHTER GREER

Creative Publishing
international

Creative Publishing
international

Copyright © 2009
Creative Publishing international, Inc.
400 First Avenue North, Suite 300
Minneapolis, Minnesota 55401
1-800-328-0590
www.creativepub.com

Printed in Singapore

10 9 8 7 6 5 4 3 2 1

Library of Congress
Cataloging-in-Publication Data

Price, Pat.
  Greenhouses & garden sheds : inspiration,
information & step-by-step projects / Pat Price ;
with Nora Richter Greer.
      p. cm.
  Summary: "Provides step-by-step photos and instructions for a variety of building projects involving and
relating to greenhouses and potting sheds"--Provided
by publisher.
  Includes index.
  ISBN-13: 978-1-58923-437-6 (soft cover)
  ISBN-10: 1-58923-437-5 (soft cover)
 1. Greenhouses--Design and construction.
2. Potting sheds--Design and construction.
I. Greer, Nora Richter. II. Title. III. Title:
Greenhouses and garden sheds.

  SB416.P75 2008
  690'.8924--dc22

2008034555

President/CEO: Ken Fund
VP for Sales & Marketing: Kevin Hamric

Home Improvement Group

Publisher: Bryan Trandem
Managing Editor: Tracy Stanley
Senior Editor: Mark Johanson
Editor: Jennifer Gehlhar

Creative Director: Michele Lanci-Altomare
Senior Design Managers: Jon Simpson, Brad Springer
Design Managers: James Kegley

Lead Photographer: Steve Galvin
Photo Coordinator: Joanne Wawra
Shop Manager: Bryan McLain
Shop Assistant: Cesar Fernandez Rodriguez

Production Managers: Linda Halls, Laura Hokkanen

Page Layout Artists: Tiffany Laschinger/ Jessica Hannon
Illustrations: Robert Leanna II
Photographer: Andrea Rugg
Shop Help: Charlie Boldt, Scott Boyd, Dave Hartley
Copy Editor: Ami Johnson
Technical Editor: Karen Ruth
Photo Research: Betsy Gammons

Contents

Introduction

GARDENERS ARE PASSIONATE. WE REJOICE when seedlings push their green tips through the soil. We revel in the scent of jasmine on a summer evening. We are persistent in our struggle with garden pests and the weather, carefully picking aphids from tomatoes and protecting lettuce plants from frost. We water, we fertilize, we coax, we coddle. And as flakes of snow descend on our barren backyards, many of us yearn for the opportunity to garden year-round in a greenhouse.

What avid gardener hasn't dreamed of bending the rules of nature just a bit, starting spring a little earlier, extending summer into October, or creating a tropical paradise in the coldest of locales? What could be more satisfying than thumbing your nose at the wind and rain from the warm embrace of a greenhouse?

Gardening structures have fallen in and out of fashion since the days when they were essentially dung-filled pits covered with mica. Today they are widely available in a variety of styles and sizes to match just about any budget. New materials and methods have reduced the costs of constructing, heating, and maintaining greenhouses, and kits are making them ever easier to build. But a wealth of choices leads to a host of questions: What style should I choose? What design is best suited to my property? How big should it be? Do I need a greenhouse, or will a garden shed do?

In the following chapters, you'll learn how to decide what type of structure is right for your needs, where and how to build it, what materials to use, and how to maintain it. You will see clear step-by-step photos of several structures as they're built, along with complete instructions for many easy-to-make accessories. Best of all, you'll find inspiration on pages packed with photos, designs, and ideas to ignite your imagination.

GREENHOUSES IN HISTORY

Gardening under glass is not a new concept. As far back as the first century A.D., the Romans, whose achievements included aqueducts, straight roads, and toilets with running water, were experimenting with growing vegetables and fruit in *specularia*—rudimentary greenhouses clad in thin sheets of mica. But the popularity of these structures declined along with the Roman Empire, and greenhouses didn't reappear until much later, with the northern European countries' first attempts at indoor gardening.

Italy and France developed the first protected gardens in the 1600s (although the French were reportedly forcing flowers in glass structures as early as 1385), and the Dutch and the British soon followed suit. By the 17th century, explorers were bringing home hundreds of exotic plant species, including citrus trees, and the British were eager to grow them. They invented the orangery, an unheated structure with a solid roof and glass walls that was designed to protect precious orange and lemon trees from frost in the winter and served as a social gathering place in the summer, when the trees were moved out into the garden.

Britain's first conservatories were also built at this time, largely for the benefit of scientists, whose main interest was in growing plants for medicinal and research purposes. In the mid-1800s, the aristocracy began to build huge glass-and-wrought-iron structures, such as the Palm House at the Royal Botanic Gardens at Kew and the Great Conservatory at Chatsworth. Soon every wealthy landowner had to have a conservatory, not just to house exotic palm trees and plants but to entertain guests and provide secluded meeting places for lovers. After the tax on glass was abolished in 1845 and the fantastic Crystal Palace was built for the Great Exhibition in 1851, greenhouses and conservatories became all the rage in Britain.

Their popularity waned, however, during World War I. As gardeners went off to battle and heating costs became prohibitive, conservatories fell victim to rust and neglect. Even the conservatory at Chatsworth succumbed; too expensive to maintain, it was demolished in 1920. But times change, and technological advances and new architectural designs have made modern greenhouses desirable, practical, and affordable, even for budget-conscious gardeners.

The Greenhouse Family Tree

Garden structures can go by many names, although strictly speaking each has a particular definition.

⬥ Conservatory. A large glass-enclosed structure designed expressly as a museum and showcase for living plants. Originally built and enjoyed only by aristocrats in Europe in the 1600s and 1700s, most conservatories today are public structures that offer everyone an opportunity to enjoy protected gardens.

⬥ Orangery. A conservatory or large greenhouse dedicated especially to the growing of citrus trees. They first appeared at the height of conservatory popularity in the 1800s.

⬥ Greenhouse. Essentially small, private conservatories, greenhouses are utilitarian structures that exist primarily for the practical propagation of plants. Glass walls allow for tender plants to germinate and grow until weather conditions are suitable for outdoor planting.

⬥ Potting shed. Sometimes called a garden shed, a potting shed isn't so much for the active growing of plants, but rather is a place for the practical work of gardening. Usually made of wood or stone rather than glass.

⬥ Sunroom. Typically a dedicated space within the architectural footprint of the house proper. Plentiful windows and lighting make the sunroom an ideal place to grow indoor plants. Less often, a sunroom serves as a kind of indoor greenhouse for starting plants that will eventually find their way outdoors.

OPPOSITE Greenhouses for private landscapes owe their heritage to the vast enclosed conservatories that began springing up in England in the 1700s and 1800s. This conservatory at Kew is a world–famous tourist destination, and its design has influenced thousands of private greenhouses.

GREENHOUSE OR GARDEN SHED: WHICH ONE IS FOR YOU?

A greenhouse, also called a glasshouse, is a framework sheathed in glass or plastic to allow in as much light as possible and to provide a controlled environment for nurturing plants. It is a functional space, designed to offer the ideal amounts of light, humidity, and warmth for propagating seeds, growing vegetables and flowers, or coaxing orchids into bloom. A greenhouse can be a small lean-to that shares an outside wall with the home or a freestanding structure that takes center stage in your garden.

If you don't have the time or budget to devote to a greenhouse, a garden shed might be the answer. Styles range from small utilitarian sheds with just enough room for starting seeds and storing tools to more spacious miniature cottages.

Regardless of the type of structure you choose, your options are limited only by your imagination. The following pages will help you to envision the possibilities and create the gardening haven you've always wanted.

TIP Dream Big, But Real

You dream of gardening indoors, but how do you choose the type of structure? Define your options; then assess your needs—and your budget—to find the right match.

ABOVE This classic home greenhouse provides 100 to 200 square feet of floor-space and is situated in a sunny spot near the primary residence.

OPPOSITE A rustic garden shed has many practical purposes, but it also goes a long way toward establishing a mood for your property.

CHAPTER ONE

Greenhouses

ENTER A GREENHOUSE AND YOU'VE CROSSED THE THRESHOLD of an extraordinary place. You're greeted by a profusion of flowers and the rich textures of foliage. Sweet fragrances mix with the earthy smell of soil. Diffused light shines through the misty air. In the silence, you can almost hear the plants growing. Traffic rumbles by unnoticed, and the distractions of the "real" world seem miles away.

Once the province of the wealthy, greenhouse gardening is now practiced by almost two million American homeowners, according to the American Horticultural Society. You'll find greenhouses on city rooftops and tucked into suburban gardens. No two are identical, even if they're constructed from the same kit; the contents of a greenhouse make it unique. Some house vegetables (tomatoes and cucumbers), some shelter tropicals (scheffleras and dieffenbachias), and some are home to flats of germinating begonias. A select few protect rare orchids and plants imported from exotic tropical locales. But they all serve a common purpose: a place where gardeners can lose themselves among green and growing things.

GALLERY OF GREENHOUSES

ABOVE Custom designed for author Amy Goldman, this greenhouse is completely at home on its upstate New York farm. Goldman documents the beauty of fruits and vegetables in her books *Melons for the Passionate* and *The Compleat Squash*.

OPPOSITE The sun's warmth prompted the thermostatically controlled roof vent to open on this freestanding greenhouse, which is almost lost among a profusion of flowers and greenery.

ABOVE In Sussex, England, a brick wall covered in "Penelope" roses fronts a Victorian greenhouse, which could be easily missed by a passerby.

OPPOSITE A gothic-arch-style greenhouse rests on a brick knee wall in a lush garden. Inside, shelves and a paved brick floor provide a showplace for plants.

ABOVE Painted a wild-grape color, this garden greenhouse is hard to miss. The structure is small in scale but large in attitude.

OPPOSITE Once you catch the greenhouse bug it's hard to keep from getting carried away. This roomy, L-shaped greenhouse rivals some commercial models in area.

LEFT A beautiful custom-tile floor is the highlight of this gorgeous greenhouse, although one could argue that the swing-out double doors are equally inviting.

ABOVE The intense humidity of a greenhouse in full bloom, coupled with the brilliant colors, creates a tropical environment that can be a genuine treat in colder seasons.

OPPOSITE Interior doors and wall frames offer the option of tacking sheet plastic to separate a large greenhouse into different climate zones. Note the lovely floor created by setting a combination of cobblestones and pavers into a sand base.

CHOOSING A GREENHOUSE

Greenhouses can take many forms, from simple, three-season A-frame structures to elaborate buildings the size of a small backyard. They can be custom designed or built from a kit, freestanding or attached, framed in metal or wood, glazed with plastic or glass. Spend a little time researching online greenhouse suppliers and you'll discover almost unlimited options. Although it's important to choose a design that appeals to you and complements your house and yard, you'll need to consider many other factors when making a decision. Answering the following questions will help you determine the type, style, and size of greenhouse that suits your needs.

How Will the Greenhouse be Used?

What do you plan to grow in your greenhouse? Are you mostly interested in extending the growing season—seeding flats of bedding plants early in the spring and protecting them from frost in the fall? Or do you want to grow flowers and tropical plants year-round?

Your intentions will determine whether you need a heated greenhouse. Unheated greenhouses, which depend solely on solar heat, are used primarily to advance or extend the growing season of hardy and half-hardy plants and vegetables. Although an unheated greenhouse offers some frost protection, it is useful only during spring, summer, and fall, unless you live in a warm climate.

A heated greenhouse is far more versatile and allows you to grow a greater variety of plants. By installing equipment for heating, ventilation, shading, and watering, you can provide the perfect environment for tender plants that would never survive freezing weather

How you plan to use the greenhouse will also determine its size, type, and location. If you only want to harden off seedlings or extend the growing season for lettuce plants and geraniums, a small, unheated structure covered with polyvinyl chloride (PVC) sheeting or even a cold frame—a glass- or plastic-topped box on the ground—might be all you need. If your intentions are more serious, consider a larger, more permanent building. A three-season greenhouse can be placed anywhere on your property and might even be dismantled in the winter, whereas year-round use calls for a location near the house, where utilities are convenient and you don't have to trek a long way in inclement weather.

The Cost Question

The cost of a basic freestanding greenhouse can range from the very economical (plastic sheeting and PVC hoop frame) to the surprisingly expensive (custom-designed and built). It all depends on your tastes and aspirations, and on your budget. The following real-life samples will give you a sense of the cost variations (remember, though, that prices can vary widely, depending on features and accessories you choose to include):

✧ A 5-ft. by 5-ft. pop-up mini greenhouse from one mail order source sold for $165.

✧ A small, 6-ft. by 8-ft. greenhouse with rigid polycarbonate panels sold for $795.

✧ A more spacious 8-ft. by 17-ft. rigid panel kit with motorized windows sold for $4,970.

✧ The most elaborate polycarbonate kit greenhouses we found, available by mail order, sold for $7,900 for an 11-ft. by 24-ft. structure.

✧ For a custom-designed and built greenhouse of the same size (11-ft. by 24-ft.), one homeowner recently spent $23,000—a price that could have been much higher for a greenhouse designed with ornamental metalwork or stone foundations.

✧ A 20-ft. by 30-ft. hoop kit using plastic sheeting and PVC tubing was recently available for $1,600.

✧ A full-featured lean-to greenhouse kit, 10-ft. by 10-ft. in size, sold for $5,724.

OPPOSITE: The ideal greenhouse has flexibility, combining some built-in features (like the shelves in this greenhouse) with ample open spaces so you can adjust the way the structure is used as your needs and interests change.

Do I want a Lean-to or a Freestanding Greenhouse?

Greenhouse styles are divided into two main groups: lean-tos, or attached, and freestanding. Lean-tos are attached to the house, the garage or an outbuilding, usually on a south-facing wall. An attached greenhouse has the advantage of gaining heat from the house. It's also conveniently close to plumbing, heating, and electrical services, which are required to operate a heated greenhouse.

On the downside, lean-tos can be restricted by the home's design: They should be built from materials that complement the existing structure, and a low-slung roofline or limited exterior wall space can make them difficult to gracefully incorporate. Siting can be tricky if the only available wall faces an undesirable direction. In cold climates, they must be protected from heavy snow sliding from the house roof. Lean-tos are typically smaller than freestanding greenhouses and can be subject to overheating if they aren't vented properly.

A freestanding greenhouse can be sited anywhere on the property and is not restricted by the home's design. It can be as large or as small as the yard permits. Because all four sides are glazed, it receives maximum exposure to sunlight. However, a freestanding structure is more expensive to build and heat, and depending on its size, it may require a concrete foundation. Utilities must be brought in, and it is not as convenient to access as a lean-to. Because it is more exposed to the elements, it can require sturdier framing and glazing to withstand winds.

Heated Greenhouse Environments

Heated greenhouses can be classified by three temperature categories: cool, warm, and hot. Each of these environments supports different plants and gardening activities.

Cool Minimum nighttime temperature: 45°F (7°C)

In a cool environment, you can start seeds and propagate cuttings early in the year so they will be ready for planting in garden beds at the beginning of summer. Unless your climate is mild, however, you'll probably need a propagator to provide a little extra warmth for starting seeds. Vegetables and hardy and half-hardy plants do well in this type of greenhouse. Although the temperature in a cool greenhouse is suitable for protecting frost-tender plants, their growth during winter is minimal.

Warm Minimum nighttime temperature: 55°F (13°C)

A warm greenhouse is suitable for propagating plants, raising seedlings, and growing a wide range of plants, including flowers, fruits, houseplants, and vegetables, even during the coldest months. You can sow tomato seeds in January and harvest the ripe fruits in June. Though this type of greenhouse provides a highly desirable environment for plants, heating it can be extremely costly, especially if you live in an area with long, cold winters.

Hot Minimum nighttime temperature: 65°F (18°C)

Only a few serious gardeners will invest in a hot greenhouse because it is prohibitively expensive to heat. This type of environment is ideal for growing exotic tropical plants, such as orchids, bromeliads, and ferns.

OPPOSITE Attached to the exterior wall of the house, this lean-to style greenhouse has all the features for complete growing success: running water (A); electrical service (B); a heated plant-propagation table (C); a heater (D) for maintaining temperatures on cold nights; ventilating windows (E) and sunshades (F) for reducing temperatures on hot days; drip irrigation system (G) for maintaining potted plants; a full-length potting bench (H) with storage space beneath; paved flooring (I) to retain solar heat.

How Big Should the Greenhouse Be?

Some experts recommend buying the largest greenhouse you can afford, but this isn't always the best advice. You don't want to invest in a large greenhouse only to discover that you're not up to the work it involves.

Of course, buying a greenhouse that is too small can lead to frustration if your plant collection outgrows the space. It is also much more difficult to control the temperature. One compromise is to buy a greenhouse that's one size larger than you originally planned, or better yet, to invest in an expandable structure. Many models are available as modules that allow additions as your enthusiasm grows.

When choosing a greenhouse, take into account the size of your property. How much space will the structure consume? Most of the expense comes from operating the greenhouse, especially during winter. The larger the structure, the more expensive it is to heat.

Be sure the greenhouse has enough room for you to work. Allow space for benches, shelves, tools, pots, watering cans, soil, hoses, sinks, and a pathway through the plants. If you want benches on both sides, choose a greenhouse that is at least 8 ft. (2.5 m) wide by 10 ft. (3 m) long. Give yourself enough headroom, and allow extra height if you are growing tall plants or plan to hang baskets.

How Much Can I Afford to Spend on a Greenhouse?

Your budget will influence the type of structure you choose. A simple hoop greenhouse with a plastic cover is inexpensive and easy to build. If you're handy with tools, you can save money by buying a kit, but if the greenhouse is large, requires a concrete foundation, or is built from scratch, you may need to hire a contractor, which will add to the cost.

Location is important: If you live in a windy area, you'll need a sturdy structure. Buying a cheaply made greenhouse will not save you money if it fails to protect your plants or blows away in a storm. And cutting costs by using inefficient glazing will backfire because you'll wind up paying more for heating.

How Much Time am I Prepared to Invest in a Greenhouse?

You may have big dreams, but do you have the commitment to match? Maintaining a successful greenhouse requires work. It's not hard labor, but your plants depend on you for survival. Although technology offers many timesavers, such as automated watering and ventilation systems, there's no point in owning a greenhouse if you don't have time to spend there. Carefully assess your time and energy before you build.

Unique Appeal

Some greenhouses and sheds are valued because they are clean and efficient. Some pay back purely in seedlings and produce. But others have a more intangible quality, perhaps even a treasured lineage that we cherish.

Today, almost nothing remains of Century Farm, located on a dirt road in the bluff country of Hay Creek Township of southeastern Minnesota, near the Wisconsin border. Century Farm was a small family dairy farm that vanished like so many when larger farm co-ops began to absorb little Midwestern family businesses in the 1970s and 1980s. When the farm was built in 1890, the lumber used to build the corn cribs and chicken coops, the dairy barn and pig shed, was hauled by sled from Wisconsin forests across the frozen surface of the Mississippi River. The logs were milled by a steam-powered saw mill put together on site; and a hundred years later, you could still see the rough marks of the huge circular saw blades that cut the planks.

Century Farm has now vanished, but the limestone foundation stones and weathered wooden planks that were part of the original farm buildings continue to live on as the walls of a dozen different garden sheds in suburban backyards across Goodhue County. For when the barns came down on Century Farm, the family reclaimed the lumber and offered it to friends for use in fences and garden structures, as a kind of living memento of a gentler time.

Spend time in a favorite garden building and you may feel the echo of history.

OPPOSITE A compact greenhouse is just the right scale for this small, enclosed backyard.

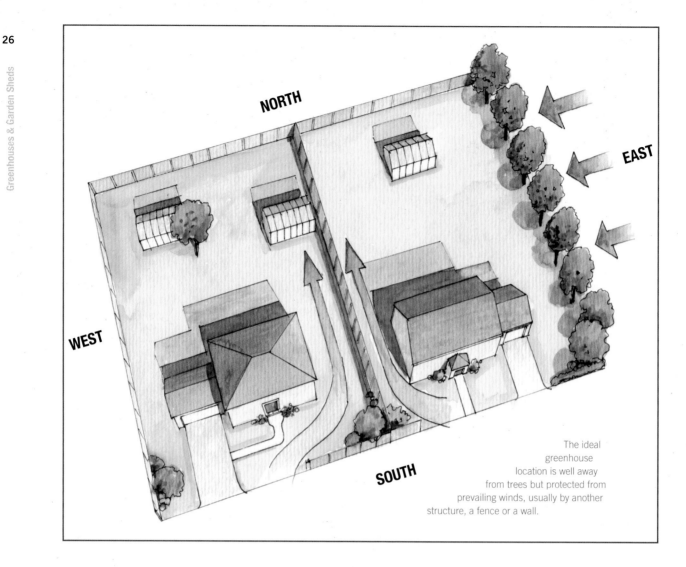

NORTH

EAST

WEST

SOUTH

The ideal greenhouse location is well away from trees but protected from prevailing winds, usually by another structure, a fence or a wall.

WHERE TO SITE YOUR GREENHOUSE

When the first orangeries were built, heat was thought to be the most important element for successfully growing plants indoors. Most orangeries had solid roofs and walls with large windows. Once designers realized that light was more important than heat for plant growth, they began to build greenhouses from glass.

All plants need at least six (and preferably 12) hours of light a day year-round, so when choosing a site for a greenhouse, you need to consider a number of variables. Be sure that it is clear of shadows cast by trees, hedges, fences, your house, and other buildings. Don't forget that the shade cast by obstacles changes throughout the year. Take note of the sun's position at various times of the year: A site that receives full sun in the spring and summer can be shaded by nearby trees when the sun is low in winter. Winter shadows are longer than those

cast by the high summer sun, and during winter, sunlight is particularly important for keeping the greenhouse warm. If you are not familiar with the year-round sunlight patterns on your property, you may have to do a little geometry to figure out where shadows will fall. Your latitude will also have a bearing on the amount of sunlight available; greenhouses at northern latitudes receive fewer hours of winter sunlight than those located farther south. You may have to supplement natural light with interior lighting.

To gain the most sun exposure, the greenhouse should be oriented so that its ridge runs east to west (see illustration, above), with the long sides facing north and south. A slightly southwest or southeast exposure is also acceptable, but avoid a northern exposure if you're planning an attached greenhouse; only shade-lovers will grow there.

Siting Factors

Several factors influence the decision of where to build your greenhouse. Some pertain to your property, some to the structure, and some to your tastes.

Climate, Shelter, & Soil Stability

Your local climate and geography have an impact on the location of your greenhouse. Choose a site that is sheltered from high winds and far enough away from trees that roots and falling branches are not a threat. (Try to position the greenhouse away from areas in which children play, too.) If you live in a windy area, consider planting a hedge or building a fence to provide a windbreak, but be careful that it doesn't cast shade on the greenhouse. Avoid low-lying areas, which are prone to trapping cold, humid air.

The site should be level and the soil stable, with good drainage. This is especially important if heavy rains are common in your climate. You might need to hire a contractor to grade your site.

Access

Try to locate your greenhouse as close to the house as possible. Connecting to utilities will be easier, and you'll be glad when you're carrying bags of soil and supplies from the car. Furthermore, a shorter walk will make checking on plants less of a chore when the weather turns ugly.

Aesthetics

Although you want to ensure that plants have the perfect growing environment, don't ignore aesthetics: The greenhouse should look good in your yard. Ask yourself whether you want it to be a focal point—to draw the eye and make a statement—or to blend in with the garden. Either way, try to suit the design and the materials to your home. Keep space in mind, too, if you think you might eventually expand the greenhouse.

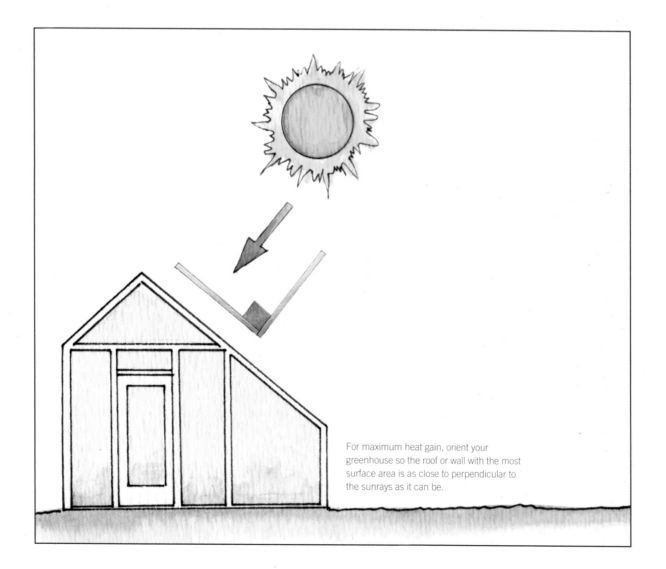

For maximum heat gain, orient your greenhouse so the roof or wall with the most surface area is as close to perpendicular to the sunrays as it can be.

GREENHOUSE STYLES

When choosing a greenhouse, consider the benefits and disadvantages of each style. Some offer better use of space, some better light transmission; others offer better heat retention, and some are more stable in strong winds. Keep in mind how you plan to use the greenhouse—its size and shape will have an impact on the interior environment.

Traditional Span

A. Ventilating roof windows

B. High gable peak provides headroom

C. 45-degree roof angle encourages runoff

D. Solid kneewalls block wind, provide impact protection and allow insulation

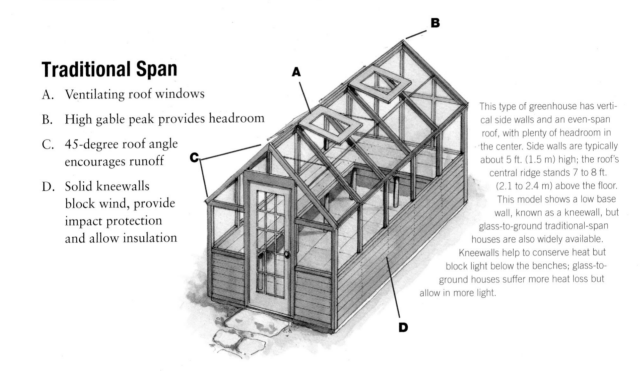

This type of greenhouse has vertical side walls and an even-span roof, with plenty of headroom in the center. Side walls are typically about 5 ft. (1.5 m) high; the roof's central ridge stands 7 to 8 ft. (2.1 to 2.4 m) above the floor. This model shows a low base wall, known as a kneewall, but glass-to-ground traditional-span houses are also widely available. Kneewalls help to conserve heat but block light below the benches; glass-to-ground houses suffer more heat loss but allow in more light.

Lean-To

A. Adjoining house provides structure and heat

B. Aluminum frame is lightweight but sturdy

C. Roof vents can be set to open and close automatically

D. Well sealed door prevents drafts and heat loss

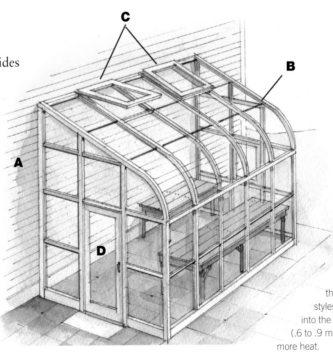

Because it is attached to the house, a lean-to absorbs heat from the home and offers easy access to utilities. This model shows curved eaves, a glazed roof, and glass-to-ground construction. Lean-tos can be built on kneewalls to provide more headroom and better heat retention than glass-to-ground styles. Sinking the foundation into the ground about 2 to 3 ft (.6 to .9 m) can conserve even more heat.

Three-Quarter Span

A. Adjoining house provides shelter

B. Half-lite door insulates but allows some light in

C. Operating side vent

D. Gable creates headroom

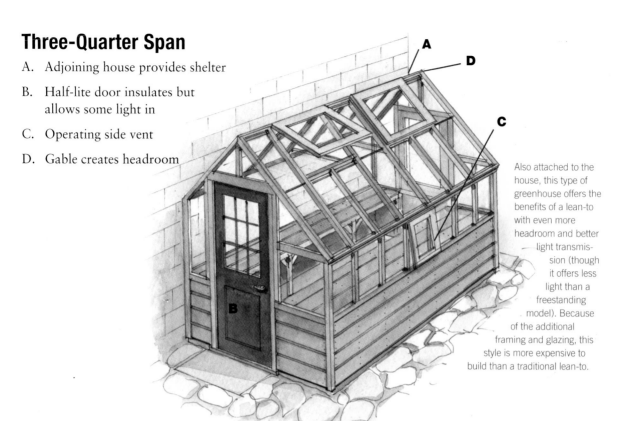

Also attached to the house, this type of greenhouse offers the benefits of a lean-to with even more headroom and better light transmission (though it offers less light than a freestanding model). Because of the additional framing and glazing, this style is more expensive to build than a traditional lean-to.

Dutch Light

A. Tapered sidewalls encourage condensation to run off

B. Lower side vent encourages airflow

C. Tile floor retains heat

D. Roof angle minimizes light reflection

Especially suitable for low-growing border crops, such as lettuce, this design has sloping sides that allow maximum light transmission. However, the large panes of glass, which may be 30 by 59 in. (77 by 150 cm), are expensive to replace.

Mansard

A. Full-width door frame

B. Sliding doors can be adjusted for ventilation

C. Lower side vents encourage airflow

D. Stepped angles ensure direct light penetration any time of day or year

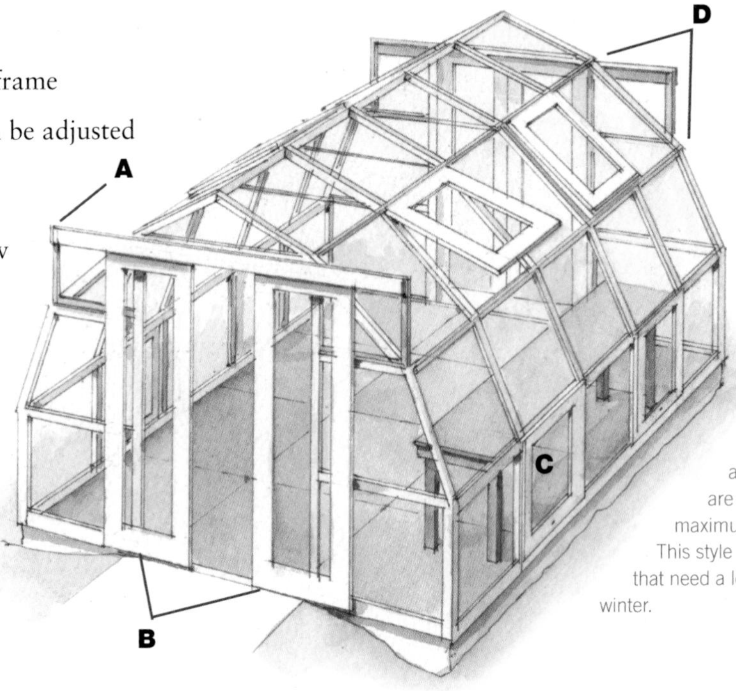

The slanting sides and roof panels that characterize the mansard are designed to allow maximum light transmission. This style is excellent for plants that need a lot of light during the winter.

Mini-Greenhouse

A. Brick wall retains heat

B. Upper shelf does not block airflow

C. Full-depth lower shelf creates hot spot below

D. Full-lite storm door

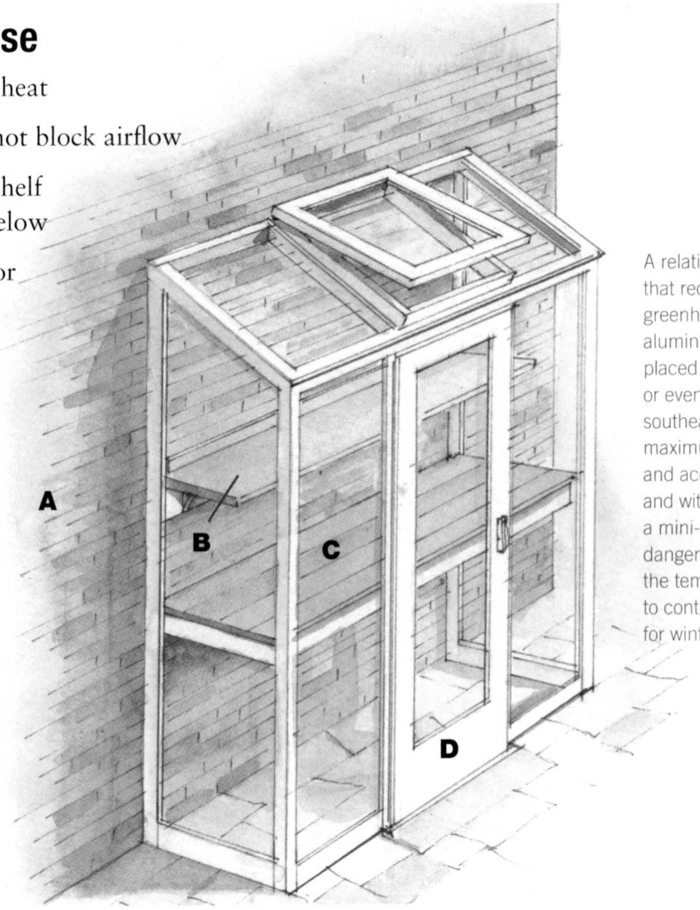

A relatively inexpensive option that requires little space, this greenhouse is typically made of aluminum framing and can be placed against a house, a garage or even a fence, preferably facing southeast or southwest, to receive maximum light exposure. Space and access are limited, however; and without excellent ventilation, a mini-greenhouse can become dangerously overheated. Because the temperature inside is difficult to control, it is not recommended for winter use.

Dome

A. Geometric dome shape is sturdy and efficient

B. Louvered air intake vent

C. Gussets tie structure together

D. Articulated door is visually interesting (but tricky to make)

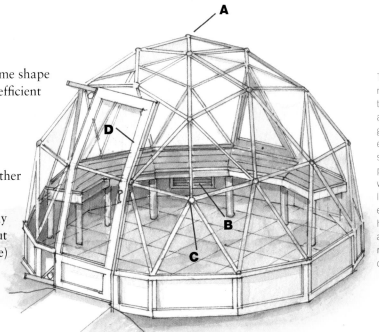

This style is stable and more wind-resistant than traditional greenhouses, and its multi-angled glass panes provide excellent light transmission. Because of its low profile and stability, it works well in exposed locations. However, it is expensive to build and has limited headroom, and plants placed near the edges may be difficult to reach.

Polygonal

A. Triangular roof windows meet in hub

B. Finial has Victorian appeal

C. Built-in benches good for planters or for seating

D. Lower wall panels have board-and-batten styling

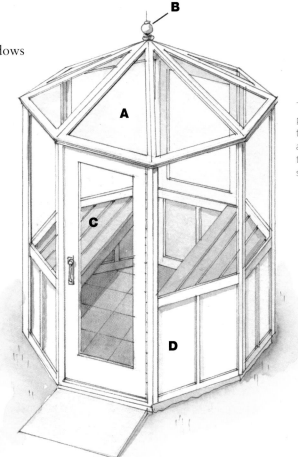

Though it provides an interesting focal point, this type of greenhouse is decorative rather than practical. Polygonal and octogonal greenhouses are typically expensive to build, and space inside is limited.

Alpine House

A. Banks of venting windows at both sides of peak

B. Adjustable louvers for air intake

C. Cedar siding on kneewall has rustic appeal

D. Fixed roof windows lend stability

Specifically designed for plants that normally grow at high elevations and thrive in bright, cool conditions, this alpine house is unheated and has plenty of vents and louvers for maximum ventilation. Doors and vents are left open at all times (except in winter). Many rock-garden plants—edelweiss, sedum, and gentian, for example—appreciate the alpine house environment.

Hoophouse

A. Bendable PVC tubes provide structure

B. 4-mil plastic sheeting is very inexpensive glazing option

C. Roll-up door

D. Lightweight base makes hoophouse easy to move

Made of PVC or metal framing and plastic glazing, this lightweight, inexpensive greenhouse is used for low-growing crops that require minimal protection from the elements. Because it does not provide the warm conditions of a traditional greenhouse, it is designed mainly for extending the growing season, not for overwintering plants. Ventilation in this style can be a problem, so some models have sides that roll up.

Conservation Greenhouse

A. High peak for good headroom

B. Louvered wall vents

C. Sturdy aluminum framing

D. Broad roof surface for maximum heat collection

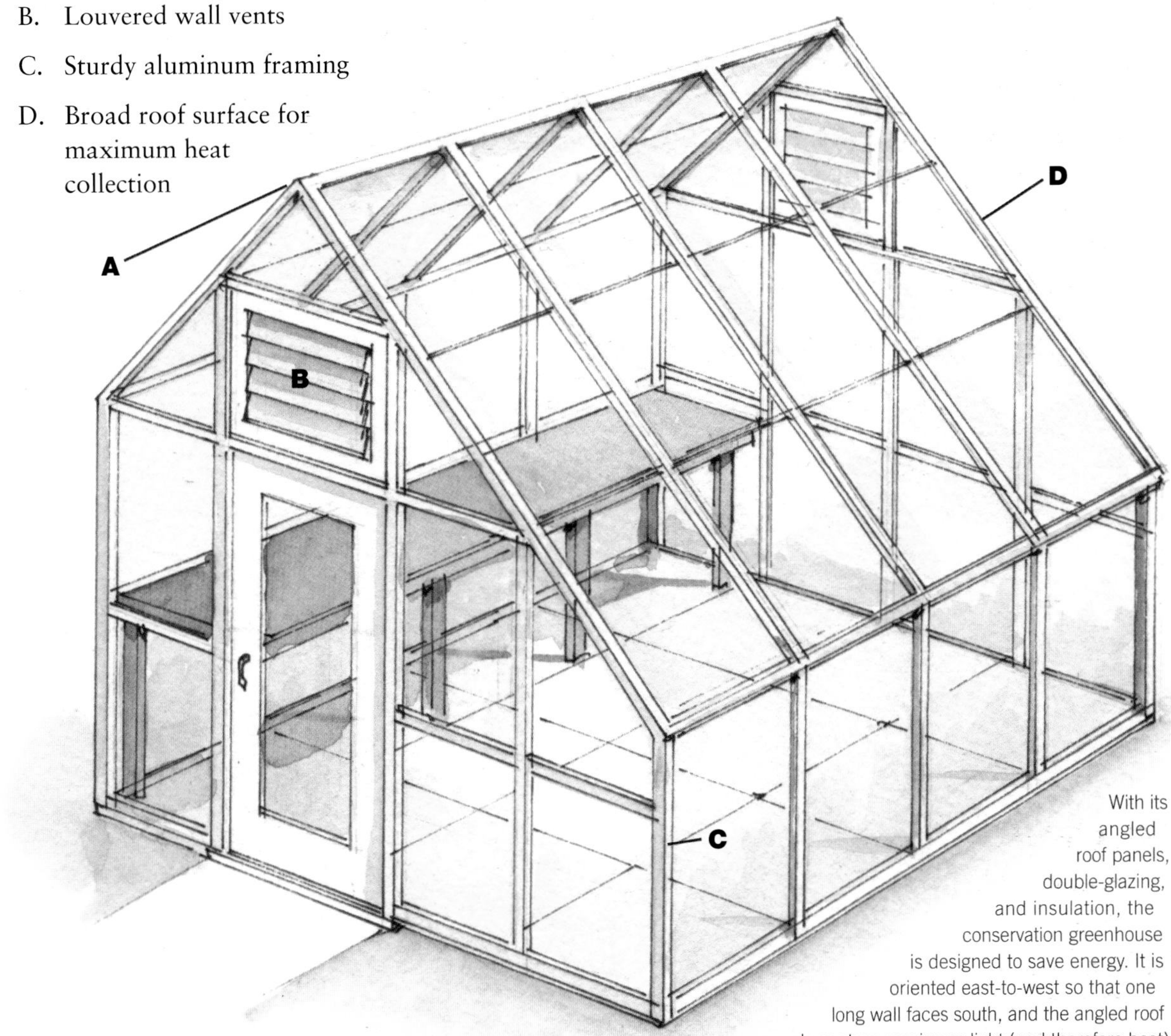

With its angled roof panels, double-glazing, and insulation, the conservation greenhouse is designed to save energy. It is oriented east-to-west so that one long wall faces south, and the angled roof panels capture maximum light (and therefore heat) during the winter. To gain maximum heat absorption for the growing space, the house should be twice as long as it is wide. Placing the greenhouse against a dark-colored back wall helps to conserve heat—the wall will radiate heat back into the greenhouse at night.

Free Greenhouse Design Software

The United States Department of Agriculture (USDA) has developed a computer software program called Virtual Grower that you can use to create your own custom greenhouse design. It helps you make decisions about roof and sidewall materials, operating temperatures, and other variables. It even has a calculator for estimating heating costs. The software can be downloaded free of charge: www.ars.usda.gov/services/software/download.htm?softwareid=108

Easy-to-Build Greenhouses

Some greenhouse designs are so simple that construction requires only a weekend or two. The foundation can be an anchored wooden frame or, for a more permanent structure, a concrete base.

Hoophouse

Economical and versatile, a hoop-style greenhouse (also called a hoophouse or a quonset house) is constructed of PVC or metal pipes that are bent into an inverted U shape, attached to a base and connected at the top by a ridgepole. A hoophouse is usually covered with plastic sheeting. A door can be set at one end, and there may be an exhaust fan or flap vent that can be rolled up for ventilation. Because the hoop greenhouse is lightweight, it is not a good choice in areas with strong winds. (For instructions on building a hoophouse, see pages 106 to 113.)

A-frame Greenhouse

An A-frame greenhouse is small and lightweight and can be made of wood or PVC. A series of A-frames is attached to a wood base and covered with plastic sheeting or rigid plastic panels, such as polycarbonate or fiberglass. Because of the steep pitch of the roof, this type of greenhouse easily sheds rain, snow, and leaves and provides more headroom than a hoop greenhouse. It can also be portable. (For instructions on building an A-frame greenhouse, see pages 114 to 121.)

A hoophouse is a simple greenhouse made by wrapping clear plastic over a series of U-shape frames. See page 106.

An A-frame greenhouse is easy to design and build yourself with just some wood and sheet plastic. See page 114.

Greenhouse Kits

No matter what kind of greenhouse you have in mind, chances are you can find a kit to match your vision. Dozens of companies offer kits in diverse styles, sizes, materials, and prices. Some offer door options—sliding versus swinging doors, for example, with and without locks and screens. Some offer glazing combinations, such as polycarbonate roof panels with glass walls. And some even offer extension kits for certain models, so you can add onto your greenhouse as your space requirements grow.

Kit basics usually include framing, glazing panels, vents (though usually not enough—it's a good idea to buy extras), and hardware. A good kit will come predrilled and precut, so you only need a few tools to assemble it. Kits do not include the foundation, benches, or accessories.

Be sure the kit you choose comes with clear, comprehensive instructions and a customer-service number for assistance. Also ensure that it complies with your local building codes and planning regulations. Depending on the company, shipping may be included in the price. Because kits are heavy, shipping can be expensive; be sure to figure it and the cost of the foundation, benches, all necessary accessories, and the installation of utilities into your budget. (For more information about constructing a greenhouse kit, see pages 96 to 105.)

This kit greenhouse has an aluminum frame and polycarbonate panels. It features sliding doors and a roof vent. With nearly 200 square feet of floor space, it was a good bargain at around $800. See page 96.

Cold Frames

An inexpensive foray into greenhouse gardening, a cold frame is practical for starting early plants and hardening off seedlings. It is basically a box set on the ground and topped with glass or plastic. Although mechanized models with thermostatically controlled atmospheres and sashes that automatically open and close are available, you can easily build a basic cold frame—or several, in a range of sizes (see Projects, page 128). Just be sure to make the back side of the frame about twice the height of the front so that the glazing can be slanted on top. Also ensure that the frame is tall enough to accommodate the ultimate height of the plants growing inside. The frame can be made of brick, plastic, or wood, and it should be built to keep drafts out and the soil in. Most important, the soil inside must be fertile, well tilled, and free of weeds.

If the frame is permanently sited, position it to receive maximum light during winter and spring and to offer protection from wind. An ideal spot is against the wall of a greenhouse or another structure. Ventilation is important; more plants in a cold frame die from heat and drought than from cold. A bright March day can heat a cold frame to 100° F (38° C), so be sure to monitor the temperature inside, and prop up or remove the cover when necessary. On cold nights, especially when frost is predicted, cover the box with burlap, old quilts, or fallen leaves for insulation.

Hotbeds

Similar in construction to a cold frame (but not as common), hotbeds have been around since Roman times. Emperor Tiberius directed his gardeners to grow cucumbers in dung-filled carts that were wheeled outside during the day and brought into a rudimentary "greenhouse" at night so that he had a supply of the vegetables year-round. This type of garden incorporates horse or chicken manure, which releases heat as it decomposes. The manure is set within the bed frame below ground level and is then topped with a layer of soil. (If you prefer, you can forgo the manure and lay heating cables between soil layers.) To prevent overheating, ventilate a hotbed as you would a cold frame.

Geraniums peek out from this well-used cold frame. The plants gain precious warmth from the brick wall, which absorbs solar heat during the day and releases it during the night.

Sunrooms

A greenhouse can certainly satisfy the desire to grow a profusion of plants year-round, but it's not everyone's cup of tea. Even the most avid gardener will agree that operating and maintaining a greenhouse requires a major commitment—in a greenhouse, the plants depend solely on you for their well-being. The sunroom, on the other hand, allows you to surround yourself with flowers and plants in a sunny, light-filled room that is designed primarily for your comfort.

Like the greenhouse, the sunroom's roots are found in the orangeries and conservatories built on the grand estates of Europe. In the 19th-century conservatory, fashionable women gathered under the glass in exotic, palm-filled surroundings for tea. The 21st-century garden room invites us to do the same, in a comfortable interior environment from which we can appreciate the outdoors year-round.

Large windows and doors open onto the terrace or garden. A high roof, which might be all glass, lets in abundant natural light. Decorative architectural features announce that this place is different from the rest of the house—separate, but in harmony. Like the conservatories of old, sunrooms can be used for growing plants and flowers indoors, but they are just as often used as sitting rooms, from which to admire the plantings outside the windows.

The sunroom can be a grand conservatory—an ornamented, plant-filled glass palace attached to an equally grand home. Or it can be a modest room containing little more than a few potted plants and a comfortable reading chair. Grand or modest, the sunroom is neither wholly of the house nor of the garden; it is a link between the two, a place in which you can feel a part of the garden but with all of the comforts of home.

Like greenhouses, sunrooms can be as simple or as elaborate as your budget and style will allow. This sunroom blends beautifully with the house.

PARTS OF A GREENHOUSE

Once you've chosen the perfect greenhouse for your property and needs, there are still many decisions to be made before you're ready to begin construction. Does it need a foundation? What type of frame and walls are best? How will you heat it or cool it? And what do you put in it? The systems you will need to operate a successful greenhouse vary with the type of greenhouse you've chosen.

Of course, once you've sorted out what you need, you will actually have to build your greenhouse. If you know your way around a tool box, and the greenhouse is relatively simple in design, you might want to consider building it yourself. But, unless you're a qualified electrician or plumber, you will probably have to hire professional help for some aspects of the construction.

Don't forget to call your municipal planning department to find out what regulations might apply in your area and whether you'll need a building permit for your greenhouse. Planning regulations and building codes regulate electrical and plumbing installation, construction (the size and strength of the frame or materials), footings and foundations, setbacks, and allowed square footage. The height of your greenhouse, in relation to existing structures, might also fall under code requirement, as can fire resistance.

A greenhouse is composed of several major systems that perform important functions. When planning your greenhouse, you'll need to make choices about each system, which include the foundation, floor, frame, glazing, ventilation, watering, heat, storage and more.

Foundations

Without a proper foundation, a greenhouse can settle and shift, damaging the frame and cracking the windows. The doors will not hang properly, and the glazing will not fit well. Even a portable, polyethylene-covered A-frame greenhouse in a sheltered yard needs a base and anchor stakes to hold it down; a large structure framed in heavy-duty aluminum or steel and glazed with glass will require a more substantial footing.

If you are building from a kit, consult the supplier to determine the recommended foundation. Many kit manufacturers supply this information with the instructions. Be sure to check with your local municipality: Building codes may require a specific foundation type.

In general, you have four foundation options: anchor stakes or earth anchors, a wood-frame, a concrete footing and walls, and a concrete slab. Regardless of the type you choose, it is critical that the foundation be square and level. Before laying any foundation, be sure you have any utility lines installed.

Using anchor stakes is the easiest and least expensive way to tie down a small greenhouse. The principle is similar to using tent pegs to hold down a tent. The greenhouse is bolted to a simple wood frame, which is held down by anchors screwed or driven into the ground. The anchors should be at least 12 in. (30.5 cm) long. Don't use this method if your site is very windy or you plan to leave the greenhouse standing during the winter. Post spikes are a similar product that can also be used for temporary greenhouses with 4x4 post support.

Kneewalls

Kneewalls are low walls to which a greenhouse frame can be attached. They can raise a greenhouse to maximize headroom and can help to retain heat. However, they also eliminate growing space behind the walls and below the benches. If you only plan to grow potted plants on the benches, this may not be a problem—you can use the area underneath the benches for storage.

Kneewalls can be built with concrete blocks on a concrete footing, but a more attractive option is to use stone or brick and mortar. To help integrate the greenhouse with your home, build the kneewall from materials that complement the exterior of the house.

For a stable, permanent glass greenhouse, you'll want to build either a concrete footing and walls or a concrete-slab foundation. To build a footing, dig a trench below the frost line, set forms into it, and pour in the concrete. When it hardens, you can either pour a concrete wall or build one from concrete blocks. Be sure the wall is at least 18 in. (46 cm) deep (or as deep as building codes recommend) and that it extends at least 6 in. (15 cm) above ground level. A block wall like the one above also requires a footing. The blocks can be mortared together or dry-laid and coated with a skim coat of concrete.

Sturdy, wood-frame foundations are usually built from pressure-treated beams, which are anchored to the ground using wood stakes or rebar attached to the frame. One tier of beams is sufficient for greenhouses 10 by 12 ft. (3 by 3.6 m) or smaller; greenhouses larger than this need two tiers. For a more permanent foundation, you can also attach a wood frame to concrete posts. Be sure to set the posts below the frost line if you live in an area with freezing winters. Your municipal building codes will prescribe the proper depth.

The most stable foundation is a concrete slab. As with the concrete wall, be sure it is above grade and that the slab is thick enough to resist cracking (3 to 4 in. [7.5 to 10 cm], depending on the harshness of your winters). To provide drainage, either slope the foundation slightly toward the edges or install a drain and a pipe that leads away from the greenhouse or connects to a sewer line. When you pour a concrete foundation, be sure to add a layer of polystyrene board insulation between the concrete and the soil to help reduce heat loss.

Floors

Even if your greenhouse is small or temporary, a dirt floor is not recommended. It will be muddy and invite weeds, diseases, and pests, making the greenhouse unpleasant, unattractive, and unsafe. If you want to save money on flooring, pea gravel is a good choice. The gravel (or any equivalent loose material) is laid several inches thick over a weed barrier (landscape fabric, not plastic) and provides excellent drainage, increases humidity when wet, and retains heat. You can also use white landscaping gravel, which has the added advantage of reflecting light.

Many greenhouse owners use an attractive combination of pea gravel and pavers, bricks, or stones. Pea gravel is laid under the benches, and the pavers, bricks, or stones are used for the greenhouse path. The pavers are set into a layer of leveled sand, and then more sand is swept into the cracks. Setting the bricks, pavers, or stones into mortar is an option that creates a more permanent pathway. You might also choose to use brick, pavers, or stone for the entire floor. As with gravel, be sure to lay down a weed barrier first.

Of course, if you've chosen a concrete-slab foundation, your greenhouse will have an easy-to-clean floor that's level and stable for benches. To make it more attractive, you can add tint, which is available in various colors, to the concrete mix. The right tint can make a concrete floor look like terra cotta.

Because concrete floors can be slippery, especially during winter, be sure to brush the surface of the wet concrete to make it a little rough. Also make sure that the concrete slopes away from the center or into a drain.

Brick pavers can be set onto a sand bed to create a semipermanent greenhouse floor that offers drainage and looks beautiful.

Pea gravel, 3/4" river rock or trap rock

Landscape fabric

Compacted gravel base

A thick layer of gravel set onto landscape fabric and a compacted gravel base makes an efficient and easily renewed floor.

Framing Materials

Although wood and aluminum are the most popular greenhouse framing materials, other products, such as steel and PVC, are available. Each type has advantages and disadvantages, so choose the one that best suits your purposes. For example, if you plan to hang baskets or put up shelves, or if your area gets a lot of snow, you'll need to choose a sturdy material to accommodate the extra weight.

Wood

Advantages: Often the first choice for custom greenhouses, wood framing is attractive, does not transfer heat as readily as aluminum, and has fewer condensation problems. It is also sturdy and, if you use cedar or redwood, rot-resistant and fragrant. You can easily fasten shelves, hooks, and other items to a wood frame. Western red cedar and redwood are recommended, but you can also use pressure-treated wood.

Disadvantages: Wood framing requires regular maintenance, and because it is bulkier than aluminum, it casts more shadow on greenhouse plants. This type of greenhouse is also difficult to add onto as a garden expands.

Aluminum

Advantages: The foremost advantage of aluminum framing is that it is low-maintenance. It is strong, and lightweight, lasts longer than wood, and can easily accommodate different glazing systems and connectors. Aluminum is used for most greenhouse kits (see page 35) and can be powder-coated or anodized in various colors, usually brown, green, or white. Kits are typically easy to assemble and come with predrilled holes for attachments. Some manufacturers offer thermally broken aluminum framing, which sandwiches a thermal barrier between two layers of extruded aluminum to decrease heat loss.

Disadvantages: Because aluminum loses heat at a faster rate than wood, this type of greenhouse is more expensive to heat. In addition, a cheaply made frame can be too flimsy to withstand high winds or heavy snow. Aluminum framing can also present condensation problems.

Galvanized Steel

Advantages: Galvanized steel framing, mostly used for commercial greenhouses, is extremely sturdy, strong, and durable.

Disadvantages: Steel greenhouses are very heavy and expensive, not just to build but also to ship. Galvanized steel is subject to rusting if it is scratched, and the rust-resistant coating can eventually wear off.

PVC (polyvinyl chloride)

Advantages: Inexpensive and easy to assemble from a kit, PVC framing is a good choice if you are just trying your hand at greenhouse gardening. It is lightweight, does not rust, and is ideal for portable or temporary greenhouses.

Disadvantages: High winds can easily damage PVC, so it's suitable only for small greenhouses, and glazing choices are restricted to plastic sheeting.

Glazing & Covers

Greenhouse glazing falls into two categories: glass and plastic, each with strengths and weaknesses. The ideal covering lets in maximum light and deters heat loss. It should also be durable and require minimal maintenance.

Glass

Advantages: Glass is the material traditionally used for greenhouse glazing, and it remains popular today. It offers excellent light transmission, resists degradation due to ultraviolet (UV) light, and has a long lifespan. It is also nonflammable and, when layered, retains heat well. Double- and even triple-pane glass is available.

Disadvantages: Uninsulated single-pane glass offers very little heat retention. Glass is also breakable—playing children, tree branches, and hail are all threats to a glass greenhouse. For safety, tempered glass is recommended because it shatters into small, rounded "pebbles" rather than sharp, jagged pieces. Glass is heavy and requires a strong, square frame and foundation or the glass can crack. Although glass offers excellent light transmission, the light is harsh and direct, not diffused, and can easily burn plants. Insulated glass can be costly.

An aluminum frame with polycarbonate glazing

A wood frame with plastic glazing

A PVC plastic tube frame with plastic sheeting

Polycarbonate

Advantages: Polycarbonate glazing is light, strong, and shatter-resistant, and when layered, it retains heat better than glass. It is available in corrugated, double-, and triple-wall panels. Corrugated polycarbonate provides excellent light transmission—equal to that of glass—but poor heat retention. Triple-wall polycarbonate (16 mm) offers excellent insulation but reduced light transmission. Polycarbonate is impact-resistant and long-lasting (15 years or longer). Unlike glass, it transmits diffused light, which eliminates shadows on plants and protects them from burns. Using twin- or triple-wall polycarbonate roof panels can increase heat retention while still allowing good light transmission.

Disadvantages: Polycarbonate scratches easily, and double- and triple-wall panels reduce light transmission. As with other plastic coverings, polycarbonate is subject to condensation, although it can be coated to reduce this problem. Like glass, it can also be costly, especially layered panels.

Acrylic

Advantages: Acrylic offers clarity and light transmission similar to glass but is lightweight and more impact-resistant. Acrylic panels are UV-resistant and can easily be molded. The material is less expensive than polycarbonate and can be layered for extra strength and heat retention. It is easy to cut and can be shaped with ordinary hand tools. Like polycarbonate, it can be coated to reduce condensation.

Disadvantages: Acrylic is not commonly used in home greenhouses. Less expensive types of acrylic can yellow, and even UV-coated acrylic will eventually need replacement. Unless it's coated, it suffers from condensation problems.

Fiberglass

Advantages: Fiberglass has improved since its debut as a replacement for glass. It is now more UV-resistant and resists yellowing. Its light transmission is almost equal to that of glass, but unlike glass, fiberglass diffuses light. It also offers better heat retention than glass and is much more durable. Good-quality fiberglass can last 20 years.

Disadvantages: Like other plastics, fiberglass tends to have condensation problems. If corrugated fiberglass is used, dirt can accumulate in the valleys, which detracts from its appearance. Inexpensive fiberglass may have a lifespan of no more than five years.

Utilities

Your greenhouse will serve you best if you equip it with power and water. Connecting utilities can be tricky, and unless you are very experienced, it is best left to a professional. In fact, your building code might require you to hire a utilities company or licensed electrician for some aspects of the connections.

Water

If the greenhouse is situated close to the house, you can simply run a hose from the outdoor tap. However, this isn't the most practical option during winter, so you'll probably want to consider installing a permanent waterline. The best time to do this is when you're building the foundation. Be sure to lay the pipe below the frost line, and install a backflow-prevention valve to avoid contaminating your drinking water. A 3/4-in. (22 mm) pipe will provide adequate water pressure for an average-size greenhouse. The pipe should connect to a dry hydrant inside the greenhouse; if the temperature drops below freezing, the hydrant can be drained to keep the pipe from bursting. If you install a sink in the greenhouse, you also must provide drainage for the wastewater by connecting the drainpipe to a sewer line, septic system, or sump.

Power

As with the plumbing, if your greenhouse is close to the house, running power to it can be as simple as connecting a cable to a junction box inside the house. You will probably need to lay underground cables, however, so it's a good idea to plan the cable route as you plan construction. Try to route cable trenches along the foot of boundaries or the edges of a lawn, avoiding areas of the garden that will be subject to digging and cultivation. If your plans include a concrete foundation, remember to dig the trench and lay the cables before you pour it.

Electric cables need to be buried at least 2 ft. (61 cm) underground (or as prescribed by code) and laid through a standard protective sheath or conduit, at least near the points where it enters a structure. Use only outdoor-rated UF cable. Check with your utility company before you dig to avoid hitting municipal power and waterlines. You'll have a lot of water splashing around inside the greenhouse, so for safety, be sure that the greenhouse circuits are connected to a ground fault circuit interrupter (GFCI). Because working with electricity is a highly specialized and potentially dangerous job, you should consult a licensed professional, who will perform continuity tests on circuits to ensure the connections are safe and that the power sources meet local building codes.

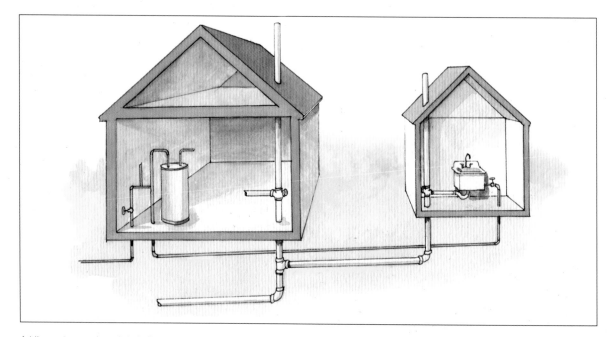

Adding water-supply and drain lines to an outbuilding is a major job requiring excavation below the frostline and other difficulties. Unless you live in an area with a shallow frostline, look for easier, more seasonal solutions, such as the project shown on pages 152 to 155.

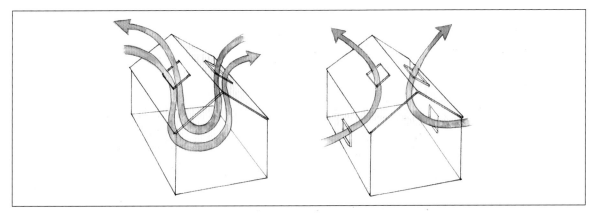

Venting your greenhouse—Installing at least one operable roof vent on each side of the ridgeline creates good air movement within the structure. Adding lower intake vents helps for cooling. Adding fans to the system greatly increases air movement.

Ventilation

Whether your plants thrive depends on how well you control their environment. Adequate sunlight is a good start, but ventilation is just as important: It expels hot air, reduces humidity, and provides air circulation, which is essential even during winter to move cold, stagnant air around, keep diseases at bay, and avoid condensation problems. You have two main options for greenhouse ventilation: vents and fans.

Because hot air rises, roof vents are the most common choice. They should be staggered on both sides of the ridgeline to allow a gentle, even exchange of air and proper circulation. Roof vents are often used in conjunction with wall vents or louvers. Opening the wall vents results in a more aggressive air exchange and cools the greenhouse much faster than using roof vents alone. On hot days, you can open the greenhouse door to let more air inside. Also consider running small fans to enhance circulation.

Vents can be opened and closed manually, but this requires constant temperature monitoring, which is inconvenient and can leave plants wilting in the heat if you are away. It's far easier—and safer—to use automatic vent openers. These can be thermostat-controlled and operated by a motor, which turns on at a set temperature, or they can be solar-powered. Unlike thermostat-controlled vent openers, which require electricity, solar-powered openers use a cylinder filled with wax, which expands as the temperature rises and pushes a rod that opens the vent. When the temperature drops, the wax shrinks and the vent closes. How far the vent opens is dictated by temperature: the higher the temperature, the wider the vent opens to let in more air.

A fan ventilator is a good idea if you have a large greenhouse. The fan is installed in the back opposite the greenhouse door, and a louvered vent is set into the door wall. At a set temperature, a thermostat mounted in the middle of the greenhouse activates the fan, and the louvered vent opens. Cool air is drawn in through the vent, and the fan expels the warm air. The fan should be powerful enough to provide a complete air exchange every 1 to 1.5 minutes.

Automatic openers sense heat build-up and open vents.

Calculating ventilation requirements

Greenhouse manufacturers rarely include enough vents in kits, so be sure to buy more. To determine the square footage of venting your greenhouse should have, multiply the square footage of the floor by 0.2.

Heating

Once you understand your greenhouse heating requirements (see Calculating Heat Needs, opposite), you'll need to determine what type of heater to use and whether you'll need to run a gas line and power to the greenhouse. The two main types of greenhouse heaters are electric and fuel-fired (gas, propane, kerosene, or oil).

Electric heaters are inexpensive and easy to install. They provide adequate heat for a small greenhouse in a temperate climate and are useful for three-season greenhouses. However, they are expensive to operate (although relative costs are constantly changing) and do not provide sufficient heat for use in cold regions. Electric units can also distribute heat unevenly, making it too warm in some areas of the greenhouse and too cold in others. Placing a heater at each end of the greenhouse can help. If you use an electric heater, be sure the fan doesn't blow warm air directly on the plant leaves; they will scorch.

Gas heaters usually cost more than electric and most areas require that a licensed professional hook them up, but heating bills will be lower than if you use an electric heater. Gas heaters operate much like a furnace: a thermostat turns on the heat when the temperature drops below its setting. You can help to distribute the heat by using a fan with the heater. If you plan to use a gas heater, install the gas line when you're building the foundation. It is also important to ensure that the heater is vented to the outside and that fresh air is available for combustion. Poor ventilation can cause dangerous carbon-monoxide buildup.

Propane, oil, and kerosene heaters also need to be vented, and if you're using kerosene, be sure it's high-grade. Another option is hot-water heating, in which the water circulates through pipes set around the perimeter of the greenhouse under the benches. You can also consider overhead infrared heat lamps and soil-heating cables as sources of heat.

In most climates, an electric heater with an automatic thermostat will be sufficient to protect tender plants on cold nights. Electricity is an expensive heating option, however, so it's best reserved for moderate heating needs.

A portable space heater may be all the supplemental heat your greenhouse requires. Use it with caution, and make sure yours shuts off automatically if it overheats or is knocked over.

Calculating Heat Needs

Heat is measured in British thermal units (Btu), the amount of heat required to raise one pound of water one degree Fahrenheit. To determine how many Btu of heat output are required for your greenhouse, use the following formula:

Area (the total square footage of the greenhouse panels) x **Difference** (the difference between the coldest nighttime temperature in your area and the minimum nighttime temperature required by your plants) x **1.1** (the heat-loss factor of the glazing; 1.1 is an average) equals **Btu**.

Calculate the area by multiplying the length by the height of each wall and roof panel in the greenhouse and adding up the totals. Here's an example, using 380 sq. ft. for the greenhouse area and 45° F as the difference between the coldest nighttime temperature (10° F) and the desired nighttime greenhouse temperature (55° F). 380 sq. ft x 45 x 1.1 = 18,810 Btu.

If the greenhouse is insulated or uses double-glazed glass or twin-wall polycarbonate, you can deduct 30 percent from the total Btu required; if it's triple-glazed, deduct 50 percent. You can deduct as much as 60 percent if the greenhouse is double-glazed and attached to a house wall.

Heating Requirements

- ◇ Oil, gas, kerosene, and other fuel-operated heaters must be vented to the outside and have a source of fresh air for combustion.

- ◇ Heaters must be equipped with an automatic shut-off switch.

- ◇ Position several thermometers at bench level throughout the greenhouse so you can check that heat is evenly distributed.

- ◇ Do not place thermometers or thermostats in direct sunlight.

- ◇ Install an alarm to warn you if the temperature drops dangerously low. Set the temperature warning high enough to give you time to remedy the problem before plants die.

- ◇ Use a backup generator to supply power to electric heaters during power outages.

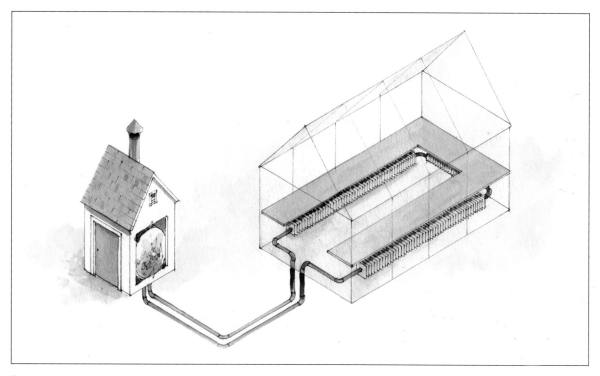

The stove for a wood-fired heating system is normally located in a remote spot near the greenhouse. In a typical set-up, the wood stove heats water that is pumped through a pipe into the greenhouse and distributed through a series of radiators.

Conserving Heat

On cold, cloudy days and at night, solar heat is lost. Even if you have supplemental heating, holding onto that heat is essential to maintaining an optimal climate. Insulating the greenhouse and making use of heat sinks are the most effective means of conserving heat, but don't overlook heat thieves such as cracks and gaps. Be sure the glazing is tight, and seal any opening that lets in cold air.

If you built a concrete foundation, it may have polystyrene board installed between the concrete and the soil. Concrete rapidly loses heat if the ground around it is cold, and polystyrene insulation helps to reduce this heat loss. You can use polystyrene board or bubble insulation (similar to bubble wrap used for shipping) to temporarily insulate the walls of the greenhouse: Simply attach the material to the greenhouse frame beneath the benches before winter and remove it in the summer. You can also insulate the greenhouse from the outside. Plant low-growing plants around the foundation, or prop hay bales or burlap bags filled with dry leaves against the walls.

Heat sinks

Heat sinks absorb solar energy during the day and radiate it back into the greenhouse at night. Stone, tile, and brick floors and walls are good collectors of heat, but to be really effective, they should be insulated from underneath. Piles of rocks can act as heat sink, but the best option is a blue- or black-painted barrel or drum full of water. Place a few of them around the greenhouse. If you have an attached greenhouse, painting the house wall a dark color can cause it to radiate solar heat back into the greenhouse at night. A light-colored wall, on the other hand, can help reflect heat and light back into the greenhouse during the day.

This heat sink system uses solar energy to heat the greenhouse. Air heated by the sun is drawn in by the fan and blown into the rock pile, which also absorbs solar heat. Heat is radiated back into the greenhouse after the sun goes down.

Smart Heat Conservation

✧ Reduce the temperature by 5°. Growth may be slowed, but plants will survive.

✧ Make sure the greenhouse is as airtight as possible.

✧ To prevent drafts, add a storm door.

✧ Mulch the soil in raised benches to insulate it during cool seasons, consider watering tropical foliage plants and other warm-season plants with water warmed to 65° F (18° C).

✧ Insulate all water- or steam-heating supply lines.

✧ At night, hang black cloth horizontally from the greenhouse ceiling as close to the plants and benches as possible to prevent the warm air from escaping through the roof.

✧ If the greenhouse uses automatic vents that are controlled by a separate thermostat, set that thermostat 5° or 10° higher than the heater thermostat to keep the vents from opening when the heat is on.

✧ Install an alarm system that will go off when the temperature goes above or below the safe range or when there is a power failure.

✧ Make use of the heat exhausted by your clothes dryer by running the vent into your greenhouse.

✧ Plant a "shelter belt" of evergreens on the windward side of the greenhouse to reduce heating costs. (But be sure it is far enough away that it doesn't cast shade on the greenhouse.)

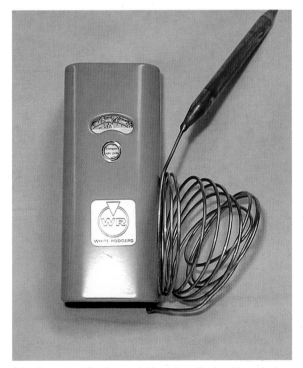

A heating and cooling thermostat is perhaps the most important greenhouse control device.

Roof vents that are triggered to open automatically by sensor alerts are far and away the most important component of a greenhouse cooling system. But additional cooling devices may be necessary.

Cooling

Although vents and fans are the first line of defense when the temperature inside the greenhouse starts to climb, other cooling methods such as misting, humidifying, evaporative cooling, and shading can also help to maintain the ideal growing environment. Cooling is crucial during summer, but it can be just as important on a sunny winter day.

Shades

By blocking direct sunlight, shades protect plants from sunburn and prevent the greenhouse from getting too hot. They can be installed on the exterior or hung from cables inside the greenhouse. Both methods block the sun, but only exterior shades prevent solar energy from penetrating the glazing, thereby keeping the air inside the greenhouse cooler.

When choosing shades, be sure they are UV-stabilized for longevity.

Two types of shades are available: cloth and roll-up. Shade cloth is usually woven or knitted from fiberglass or polyethylene and is available in many colors, although green, black, gray, and white are most common. You can also find shade cloth in silver, which, like white, reflects heat and sunlight and keeps the greenhouse cooler than darker colors. Shade cloth also varies in density, usually from 20 percent to 80 percent. The higher the density of the cloth, the more light it blocks (60 percent density blocks 60 percent of the light). Be careful when choosing shade density; too little light will slow plants' growth.

Shade cloth can be simply thrown over the greenhouse and tied down when shading is needed, but this hampers airflow through the vents (unless you cut the cloth to size and install it in sections). Better ventilation is achieved by suspending the cloth 4 to 9 in. (10 to 23 cm) above the exterior glazing. Be sure the vents are open when you do this. Greenhouse shade suppliers can provide framework kits.

Roof shades, along with vents, help prevent a greenhouse from overheating in direct sunlight. Here, a combination of circulating fans and cloth shades mounted on the interior of the south-facing glass helps protect plants.

Louvered and roll-up shades help to block the sun in this greenhouse.

In addition to cloth, roll-up greenhouse shades may be constructed from aluminum, bamboo, or wood. They are convenient because you roll them up when they're not needed, and they last longer than shade cloth, but they are more expensive.

Evaporative Coolers

Evaporative coolers (also called swamp coolers) cool the air by using a fan to push or pull air through a water-saturated pad. A portable cooler might be sufficient for a small greenhouse; larger greenhouses will benefit from a unit cooler placed outside. Used when the humidity outside is less than 40 percent, these units draw dry outside air through the saturated pad, where it is cooled. The air travels through the greenhouse and exits via a vent on the opposite side. It's a good idea to use an algaecide with these coolers.

Liquid Shading

Some greenhouse gardeners choose to paint liquid-shading compounds (sometimes called whitewashing) over the outside glazing. These compounds are inexpensive and easy to apply, but they can be unattractive and tend to wash off in the rain. Liquid shading can be thinned or layered to the level desired, and the residue can be brushed off at the end of summer. (It is often almost worn off by that point anyway). Some liquid-shading compounds become transparent during rainy weather to let in more light and then turn white when they dry.

Microclimates

When you landscape your property, you consider its microclimates: the sunny, sheltered corner; the cool, shady spot beneath the trees; that strip along the back that always catches the breeze. Your greenhouse has microclimates, too: It's warmer near the roof and cooler at floor level; some spots are shaded and others receive strong, direct light; and down near the wall vents, it's cool and breezy. Like the plants in a garden, greenhouse plants have differing light, heat, soil, and moisture requirements. Before you place them in the greenhouse, take stock of its microclimates, and group plants according to their needs.

Although this system is in a large commercial greenhouse, similar programmable overhead watering systems can be used in smaller private greenhouses.

Watering & Misting

If your greenhouse is fairly small and you enjoy tending plants daily—pinching off a spent bloom here, propping up a leaning stem there—you might enjoy watering by hand, either with a watering can (which is laborious, no matter how small the greenhouse) or with a wand. Hand-watering helps you to pay close attention to plants and cater to their individual needs. You'll quickly notice signs of over- or under-watering and can adjust accordingly.

However, hand-watering isn't always practical. Many gardeners use an automatic system such as overhead sprinkling and drip irrigation. This approach is convenient, especially when you are out of town, and it lets you meet individual plant-watering needs if you group those with similar requirements together. Greenhouse suppliers sell kits as well as individual parts for automated watering systems. Be sure your system includes a timer that can be set to deliver water at specific times of the day, for a set duration, and on specific days of the week. You can also incorporate water heaters and fertilizer injectors into your system.

Overhead-sprinkler systems are attached to the main water supply and use sprinkler nozzles connected to PVC pipes installed above the benches. The system usually includes a water filter, which prevents the nozzles from clogging, and a pressure regulator. Set the system to water in the morning and during the hottest part of the day. Avoid watering late in the day so the plants will be dry before nightfall, when the temperature drops and dampness can cause disease.

Drip-irrigation systems use drip emitters to water plants slowly, a drop at a time, when moisture is needed. Each plant has an emitter attached to feeder lines that connect to a drip line of PVC tubing or pipe, which runs along the benches and back to the main water supply. Unlike overhead sprinklers, drip irrigation ensures that the plant leaves stay dry. It also helps to conserve water.

If you prefer to water plants from underneath, consider capillary mats. These feltlike mats are placed on top of the bench (which is first lined with plastic) and under the plants, with one end of the mat set into a reservoir attached to the bench. The reservoir ensures that the mat is constantly moist.

Moisture from the mat is drawn up into the soil and to the plant roots when water is needed. Unlike drip irrigation and overhead sprinkling, capillary-mat watering systems do not require electricity, pipes, or tubing. However, unless they are treated, the mats will need regular cleaning to prevent mildew and bacteria buildup. To ensure that the system works properly, it's important that the bench be level.

Regardless of the watering system you choose, use lukewarm water. Cold water can shock the roots, especially if the soil is warm. If you're hand-watering, let the water sit in the greenhouse so it warms up to ambient temperature. (Keep it out of the sun, though—you don't want it to get too hot). Wand watering and automatic systems can benefit from an installed water heater.

Misting

When the temperature inside the greenhouse rises and the vents open, they release humidity. Misting increases humidity, which most plants love—levels of about 50 percent to 65 percent are ideal—and dramatically decreases the temperature by as much as 20° F (6° C). Misting systems are available through greenhouse suppliers. You can buy a complete system, which might include nozzles, tubing, PVC pipe, a humidistat, and sometimes a hard-water filter and a pressure gauge, or you can buy the parts separately to create a customized system. The size of the greenhouse will determine the size of the system: Larger greenhouses need more nozzles and in turn more tubing and pipe.

Humidistats can automatically turn on misters and humidifiers when the humidity drops below a set level. You might also want to invest in a device to boost the water pressure. Higher pressure produces a finer mist, which cools more quickly. Suppliers recommend placing the nozzles about 2 ft. (6m) apart around the perimeter of the greenhouse, between the wall and the benches. Place the nozzles underneath the benches so the mist doesn't drench the plants. As with watering, avoid misting late in the day. Wet leaves and cold, humid air can encourage disease.

Misting systems restore the ambient humidity that is released when greenhouse vents open during the heat of the day. A humidistat monitors moisture levels and controls the misting system.

Lighting

If you've placed your greenhouse in a sunny, south-facing location, well away from shade, plants should get adequate sunlight during the summer. But if the greenhouse faces north or is shaded during the day, plants may need additional light. And no matter where the greenhouse is located, you'll likely need to rely on supplemental lighting during winter.

Supplementing natural light with artificial light can be tricky. Natural light is made up of a spectrum of colors that you can see (the red, orange, yellow, green, blue, indigo, and violet colors of the rainbow) and those you can't see (infrared and ultraviolet). Plants absorb light from the red and blue ends of the spectrum—blue light promotes plant growth; light from the red end of the spectrum encourages plants to flower and bud. The red-blue light combination is easily achieved when the source is the sun but a little more difficult when you're using artificial lighting. Intensity is also important: Lights that are set too far away or that don't provide enough brightness (measured in lumens or foot-candles) will produce weak, spindly plants.

Three basic types of lights are available: incandescent bulbs, fluorescent tubes, and high-intensity discharge (HID) lights, which include metal halide (MH) or high-pressure sodium (HPS). Each has advantages and disadvantages, which is why greenhouse gardeners often use a combination of two or more types to achieve light that is as close to natural as possible.

Incandescent

Ordinary tungsten incandescent bulbs are inexpensive, readily available, and a good source of red rays, but they are deficient in blue light. They can be useful for extending daylight for some plants and for supplementing low light levels, but they are not an efficient primary source of light. Incandescent lights produce a lot of heat—hanging them too close to plants can burn foliage, but if you hang them at a safe distance, they don't provide enough intensity for plant growth. The average life span of an incandescent bulb is about 1,000 hours.

If you plan to operate your greenhouse between late fall and early spring, you will need to provide both heat and light.

Fluorescent

Fluorescent tubes are more expensive than incandescent bulbs, but the higher cost is offset by their efficiency—bulb life for fluorescents is about 10,000 hours. They shed little heat and are available in a variety of colors, including full-spectrum light. Cool-white fluorescents, which produce orange, yellow-green, blue, and a little red light, are the most popular choice. Combining fluorescent tubes with incandescents increases the amount of red light available to plants, but you will have to hang two types of fixtures. The downside to using fluorescent lights is that they must be hung very close to plants (within 6 to 8 in. [15–20 cm]) to be effective. They're most useful for propagation and for low-growing plants.

HID

High-intensity discharge (HID) lights work by sending an electrical charge through a pressurized-gas tube. There are two types: high-pressure sodium (HPS), which casts light in the yellow, orange, and red end of the spectrum, and metal halide (MH), which leans more toward the blue end, casting blue/violet light. MH lamps are often recommended as the primary light source for greenhouse growing, with HPS lights as a secondary light source. MH light mimics spring light and encourages early plant growth; HPS light resembles the type cast by the sun during fall and promotes fruiting and flowering. Greenhouse gardeners often start plants out under MH lamps and then switch to HPS. This requires switching fixtures during the growing season, which can be a nuisance. Convertible fixtures house both types of bulbs so that they can be used in tandem or succession.

HID lights are very expensive, but their lifespan is long: A standard 400-watt bulb can last 20,000 hours. They also cover a large area: a 400-watt lamp lights 16 sq. ft. (1.5 sq. m) of space. HID lights produce heat, so they should be hung higher in the greenhouse. If you use them, be sure to provide plenty of ventilation during summer.

TIP Lighting Considerations

The best lighting for growing greenhouse plants mimics natural light. Invest in lamps that resemble natural light in intensity and quality (or color), and use them when days are short or cloudy.

Fluorescent is a better source of growth-stimulating light for your greenhouse. It must, however, be hung relatively close to plants in order to benefit their growth.

Ordinary incandescent lights aren't particulary good sources of growth-promoting light, but they can help heat a greenhouse. And their attractive warm light also turns a greenhouse into a nighttime landscape design feature.

Benches and Storage

Every greenhouse needs benches to support plants and provide space for potting. Because plants can be heavy, it's important that benches be sturdy.

How you lay out benches depends on your needs and the size of your greenhouse. Most average-size greenhouses can accommodate a bench along each wall, with an aisle down the middle for access. If you have enough space along one end wall, you can install more benches to create a U shape. Another option is to arrange the benches in a peninsula pattern. Shorter benches are set at right angles to the outside walls, with narrow aisles in between, leaving space for a wider aisle down the middle. You can also use a single, wider bench along a side wall and leave space for portable benches and taller plants against the other wall. A larger greenhouse can accommodate three benches with two aisles.

Regardless of the layout you choose, it's best to orient benches along a north-south line so plants receive even light distribution throughout the day. Use the space as efficiently as possible, and don't inadvertently block the door. Allow enough room in the aisles to move around comfortably; make them wider if you need to accommodate a garden cart or wheelbarrow. Set benches about 2 in. (5 cm) from the greenhouse walls to provide airflow, and avoid placing benches near any heat source.

Bench width is determined by the length of your reach, so if you are short, you may want benches to be narrow. The same concept applies to height: Although the average bench is about 28 to 32 in. (71 to 81 cm), yours can be higher or lower to suit your height and reach. (If they need to be wheelchair-accessible, lower them even more.) If you have access to benches from both sides, you can double their width.

Several options are available for bench tops. Wood slats are sturdy and attractive, and they provide good drainage and airflow. Be sure to use pressure-treated or rot-resistant wood, such as cedar, keeping in mind that cedar benches can be expensive. Wire mesh costs less, is low-maintenance, and also provides good airflow, but be sure that it is strong enough to support heavy plants. Plastic-coated wire-mesh tops are available. These are similar to (if not the same as) the closet shelving found in home stores. Usually white, they have the advantage of reflecting light within the greenhouse.

Sturdy benches that are easy to clean and withstand moisture are a critical part of a greenhouse that's pleasant to work in.

For space efficiency, potting benches can double as storage containers. Here, the potting benches include spaces for mixing and storing soils for potting. Slatted covers make it easy to keep the bench-tops tidy.

You can also choose solid tops made of wood, plastic, or metal. Solid wood tops should be made from pressure-treated wood, and metal tops should be galvanized to prevent rust. Solid tops provide less air circulation than slatted or mesh tops, but they retain heat better in winter and are necessary if you use a capillary-mat watering system.

The greenhouse framing material will determine whether you can install shelves. Shelves can easily be added to a wood-framed greenhouse, and many aluminum greenhouse kit manufacturers provide predrilled framing, along with optional accessories for installing shelves. Keep in mind that even if shelves are wire mesh, they can cast shade onto the plants below.

If you plan on potting inside the greenhouse, you can use part of the benches or dedicate a separate space for a potting bench in a shady corner or along an end wall. For convenience,

consider building or buying a potting tray that you can move around and use as needed.

Unless you have a separate place to store tools and equipment, you'll need to find room for them in the greenhouse. To determine how much space you'll need, first list all of the equipment necessary to operate the greenhouse: everything from labels, string, and gardening gloves to bags of soil, pots, trash cans, and tools. If you will use harmful chemicals, be sure to include a lockable storage area.

Just as in your home, finding storage space in the greenhouse can be a challenge. Look first to shady areas. If the greenhouse has a knee wall, the area under the benches can provide a good deal of storage space. Shelves can also provide storage space for lightweight items. Be creative and make efficient use of any area where plants won't grow to create accessible yet tidy storage for equipment.

Potting Materials

If you're a container gardener, you are already familiar with the vast array of pots available at garden centers. For greenhouse gardening, however, pot choices are narrowed to two types: terra cotta and plastic.

Terra cotta pots are attractive and heavier than plastic, which means they are less likely to be knocked over. In addition, they are porous—because water evaporates through the clay, the risk of overwatering is lower. However, you will have to water plants more often and clean the pots regularly to remove deposits caused by minerals from water and soil leaching through the sides. Glazed terra cotta pots hold moisture better than unglazed pots and don't show mineral deposits. Terra cotta pots are more expensive than plastic pots.

Practical and inexpensive, plastic pots hold moisture better than terra cotta pots, so you don't have to water plants as often. Gardeners who plan to start seeds and propagate plants often use plastic trays, flats, and cell packs, although peat pots, cubes, and plugs are also available for starting seeds.

Keep a ready supply of potting soil, peat, and any other planting amendments you may use. If you do not have a good space in your greenhouse (underneath a potting bench is a typical good spot), then consider building a garden shed nearby (see next chapter).

Terra cotta containers are preferable if your plants will live in the pot permanently. If you are only starting plants for transplant, inexpensive plastic pots and trays are a good choice.

Hydroponics

Hydroponics, the process of growing plants without soil, has become popular with greenhouse gardeners, especially for growing vegetables. Hydroponic growing medium, which holds plants in place, can be made of polystyrene balls, expanded clay pellets, gravel, pea stone, perlite, vermiculite, rock wool, or coconut fibers. The simplest method is to place growing medium into a pot and add a nutrient solution once or twice a day. A more complex system involves using computer-controlled pumps to automatically flush plants' roots with nutrient solution as necessary for maximum growth.

Lettuces are probably the most common hydroponically grown vegetable. They often are shipped with the root system intact for greater longevity.

Root systems grow through the plant support medium and down into the water below. Here, the water is contained in a child's plastic wading pool.

Many vegetables and herbs that are suitable for greenhouse growing are also good candidates for a hydroponic environment. Testing different species and judging their success can be a fun process.

GREENHOUSE MAINTENANCE

Adiseased leaf, a spot of mildew—in the warm, humid air of a greenhouse, it doesn't take much to unleash a potentially fatal fungal infection. Daily inspection and cleanup combined with more intensive seasonal and annual maintenance should keep your greenhouse running smoothly and help plants to thrive.

Greenhouse Shading Compound

Professional greenhouse growers with large operations typically apply greenhouse shading compound to the glazing of their structures so they can control heat entry and protect their plants. Similar to paint, shading compound contains ground pigments that reflect the suns rays. The compound is sprayed onto the glazing with an airless sprayer (you can use a hand-sprayer for a small greenhouse). Sold in 5-gallon buckets, it is diluted with water at an 8 to 1 ratio for plenty of coverage. Some types are designed to be easily removed with water and a fine nylon broom so you can make adjustments as needed. Other formulations are intended to be permanent. For more information, ask about the product at your greenhouse supply store or do an online search for Greenhouse Shading Compound.

Regular Maintenance

- Check the undersides of the leaves and remove pests; wash leaves.

- Clean up spills; put away hoses and water cans.

- Sweep up fallen leaves and soil; keep floors clean.

- Clean tools after using and put them away.

- Put away bags of soil, fertilizer, pots, and trays.

- Check drip irrigation lines for blockages.

- Clean mister and sprinkler nozzles.

- Regularly inspect the greenhouse for cracks, rust, or leaks; make simple repairs if needed.

- Clean glazing (dirty glazing reduces light transmission); use cleaners formulated for algae removal; clean polycarbonate glazing with mild dish detergent.

- Quarantine sick plants to keep disease from spreading; discard those that can't be nursed back to health.

- Keep the greenhouse interior as clean as possible.

- Pull and dispose of weeds.

Annual Cleaning

- Choose a warm, still day in autumn to thoroughly clean and disinfect the entire greenhouse.

- First remove all plants and place them outside or in a protected spot. Start with the inside.

- Using a 10 percent solution of household bleach in water, scrub down the benches, walls, framing, and floors. Be sure to turn off electric power first. Clean all surfaces thoroughly.

- Soak pots, trays, and containers in bleach solution, then scrub, rinse, and let dry.

- When the interior is dry, return plants to the greenhouse, first checking them for pests from outdoors.

- When the interior is done, move to the outside. Wash the glazing, framing, doors, vents, and all exterior surfaces.

- Use specially formulated cleansers for removing tree sap and other stubborn stains.

Seasonal Maintenance

Spring/Summer

- Clean gutters and screens.

- Clean glazing.

- Clean and sterilize pots and flats—replace or repair, as necessary.

- Inspect glazing, replace broken or cracked panes; recaulk, if necessary.

- Oil door hinges, clean sliding-door tracks.

- Repair loose flashing.

- Check and clean circulating fans and humidifiers.

- Touch up paint, if necessary.

- Replace rotting or damaged wood.

- Inspect and lubricate fans, louvers, and vents—repair or replace, as necessary.

- Inspect greenhouse shades for damage or wear and replace, as necessary.

- Apply shading compound, if using.

- Lubricate metal frames; check joints and connections.

Fall/Winter

- Perform annual cleaning.

- Brush off shading compound; remove and store shades.

- Weather-strip doors, seal cracks and all air leaks.

- Replace broken, cracked, or worn glazing; caulk, as necessary.

- Apply insulation.

- Check, oil, and test-run heaters—repair, as necessary.

- Clean glazing.

- Re-apply wood sealant or preservative to exterior wood framing.

- Check thermostats.

CHAPTER TWO

Garden Sheds

GREENHOUSES INSPIRE US TO THINK BIG, TO IMAGINE BUILDING our own crystal palaces. They can be showplaces for exotic blooms and botanical beauty. But they require plenty of tools and materials to maintain. If you'd prefer not to clutter your greenhouse visually or physically, build a useful garden shed to handle tool storage and other dirty work. This chapter shows you how to design and build your own garden shed. Even if you don't own or want a greenhouse, a quaint garden shed provides handy storage space and adds architectural interest in your landscape.

There is no one distinguishing factor that differentiates a garden shed from any other outbuilding, other than its proximity to your garden. It can be a classic wood shed, metal kit shed, or a prefabricated plastic shed. But the shed you choose should reflect how you feel about gardening. If you are attracted to the romance of gardening, you'll probably gravitate toward a shed with a classic roofline, wood siding or shakes, a slat-built door and a fixed sash barn window. If your interest is more utilitarian (say, you garden because you love fresh vegetables), then a metal kit shed next to the vegetable garden makes some sense.

In this chapter you'll see plenty of examples representing a wide range of sheds. For most of us gardeners, the problem isn't finding one we like, it's deciding among so many that we like.

GALLERY OF GARDEN SHEDS

ABOVE AND OPPOSITE This delightful architectural folly is actually a working garden shed. Tucked between a row of trees and a stepped slope, it sports an exaggerated polycarbonate roof that lets in plenty of light. Trellises support climbing vines on both sides of the Dutch door.

The sloping front wall of this delightfully weathered potting shed makes use of recycled windows to take advantage of sunlight. The wood walls and the door, which leads to a small storage area, are also recycled.

Details such as painted shutters and a trompe l'oeil climbing-ivy motif transform this small hip-roofed shed into a garden jewel.

Inside the shed, a bright-blue armoire displays pot and dried flowers, but it also creates an environment that most gardeners will find thoroughly pleasant as a place to sit and relax.

This hardworking shed has a humble charm that is an excellent fit with its surroundings. The fieldstone foundation wall is a perfect fit.

These gambrel sheds are practically twins. Between them, they can store all the tools needed to tend this cutting garden, and plenty more, to boot.

A basic lean-to shed packs a generous amount of storage space in a small footprint—and it doesn't have to back up to another structure.

ABOVE Small spaces are perfect for small sheds. This garden charmer has just enough space to accommodate the tools and materials needed to tend a small city garden, along with a bit of design flair that makes its presence feel larger.

RIGHT This old garden shed is rich with character and charm that bids visitors welcome and can be hard to leave behind.

ABOVE A metal kit shed may lack some of the warmth and charm of a handmade wood shed, but it provides lots of handy storage for a relatively small outlay of cash. Plus, it can be set up quickly.

RIGHT Cedar siding lends a hint of richness to this very simple shed. The double doors make it easy to push wheelbarrows and lawn mowers up the ramp and into the shed.

Simple lines and classic construction are a tough combination to beat when you're designing any garden structure. The strap hinges heighten the familiar appeal of this shed.

This unique outbuilding is part greenhouse and part shed, making it perfect for a year-round garden space or backyard sunroom, or even an artist's studio.

CHOOSING A GARDEN SHED

Not long ago, the garden shed was a strictly utilitarian structure, built from scrap lumber and hidden in a corner to serve as a cobwebbed closet for rusted rakes and hoes. If that's all you need, you can buy a standard wood or metal shed from a local home-and-garden store. But if you want more charm and style, you can find a wide variety of designs for a shed that can serve as a potting haven, art studio, home office, writer's retreat, woodworking shop, even a guest cottage. Whatever your heart desires, online suppliers offer myriad styles and accessories to give even the plainest structure your own architectural signature. And best of all, it doesn't have to cost a fortune.

With some exceptions, a garden shed isn't nearly as complex to design and build as a greenhouse. But no one wants a shack with a sagging door, so you'll need a plan. You can hire a professional to create a custom structure; buy a kit; purchase a set of plans to construct with or without professional help; or have a prefabricated shed delivered to your yard.

Some shed kits, such as this panelized cedar shed kit, are delivered directly to your house partially assembled and packed on pallets.

Anatomy of a Shed

Shown as a cutaway, the shed below illustrates many of the standard building components and how they fit together. It can also help you understand the major construction stages. Although there is no single way to build a shed, these simple structures tend to want to go together in more or less the same way. Essentially, the strategy comes down to "Build from the ground up." Here is a general sequence:

1. Foundation—including preparing the site and adding a drainage bed
2. Framing—the floor is first, followed by the walls, then the roof
3. Roofing—adding sheathing, building paper, and roofing material
4. Exterior finishes—including siding, trim, and doors and windows

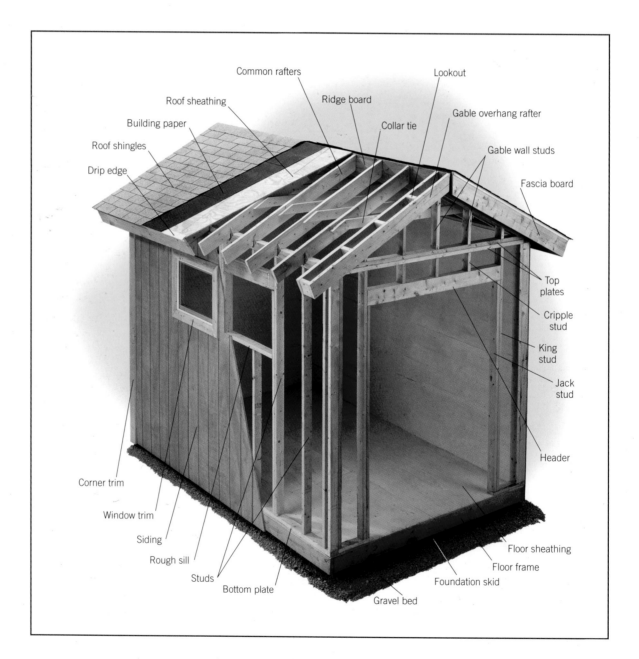

Choosing a Style

Although some five-sided shed designs are available, most sheds are rectangular or square with varying roof styles, usually saltbox, gambrel, gable, or the classic shed style (a flat roof with a slight slope). You can customize the design to match your desires. For example, if you yearn for a greenhouse but have a limited budget, you can create a "sun shed" that incorporates large panels of glazing, usually acrylic or polycarbonate, into a saltbox-style structure. The glazing allows in enough sunlight to nurture seedlings and protect frost-sensitive plants, extending the gardening season. If your climate is reasonably temperate, you can even overwinter tubers and bulbs in this type of shed.

When choosing a design, consider whether you want it to match the style of your home. If it's tucked away on the property, hidden from view, matching is unnecessary. But if you plan to place the shed near the house, its style should complement the architecture. In fact, designing it to look like a miniature version of the house—roof, siding, windows, and all—can be fun. It should at least mimic the home in color or the style of windows, for example. Avoid a mix of styles—a rustic, log-cabin-style shed will look out of place near a sleek, modern house, as will a Japanese teahouse with a Colonial-style home.

This utility shed is so small it's practically portable, but it succeeds in design because it has classic shed features, like the slightly sloping shed-style roof.

Choosing a Size

A garden shed needs space for a potting bench, tools, a wheelbarrow or mower, hoses, other landscaping paraphernalia and maybe a comfortable chair for you. To get a sense of how much space you'll need, use string and stakes to outline an area in the shed's planned construction area. Mark areas for shelving and furniture, and note the location of windows and doors. Do you have clear access to your tools and equipment? Can you move around comfortably?

Of course, the size of your property and your home will impact the scale of your shed—a disproportionately large structure will look out of place. Keep in mind that a garden shed's small size is part of its charm. And be sure to check with your municipal planning department before you finalize plans—zoning regulations can limit outbuildings' size. By keeping the size of your shed below your local code threshold, you also may be able to avoid the cost of a building permit. In many areas, for example, freestanding structures with a footprint of less than 100 square feet (9.2 sq.m) do not require a permit. (In other areas you use the square footage of the roof as a guideline.)

Choosing a Site

Where you put your shed depends in part on whether you want it to be a secluded hideaway or a focal point that draws the eye to a colorful spot in the yard. Once you've made that determination, you'll need to consider the following factors to find the ideal site.

Purpose

The purpose of the shed should weigh heavily in where it is placed. You'll want a playhouse to be close to the house; a retreat can be farther away. A potting shed should be near the garden, whereas a woodworking shop or home office will benefit from being close to the house and utility lines. If you'll be using the shed year-round, make sure it will be accessible in nasty weather.

Because its floor plan is less than 100 square feet (9.2 sq.m) in area, this shed did not need a building permit (and fee) to be built. Exact thresholds between size and permit requirements are established by your municipality.

Zoning

Zoning regulations will almost certainly influence your choice of site. Call the planning department to find out what restrictions apply in your area. In some cases, a home office or guest cottage may not be allowed. Mapping out your property can be tremendously helpful in assessing possible sites. (Be sure the map is to scale.) Mark the locations of the main house and any outbuildings as well as paved areas, fences, trees, and established plantings that you don't want disturbed. Include zoning restrictions, such as setbacks and easements, and the positions of utility lines.

Sun & Climate

Assess the sun and shade patterns on your property. If you want to grow plants in your shed, you'll need a site that will get at least six hours of sunlight. A quiet place for reading or writing might be better placed in an area that receives shade, especially from mid- to late-afternoon.

Are your summers hot and sticky? If so, orient the shed to catch breezes. If your climate is windy, however, you'll want a sheltered spot. Nearby deciduous trees can provide welcome shade during summer and allow sun to shine through in winter, when the trees are bare. But if frequent storms are the norm, placing the shed near trees probably isn't a good idea. A site near a pond or lake is picturesque and can be cooler than areas without water. Remember that sun and weather patterns change throughout the year; position a shed that you'll use year-round with this in mind.

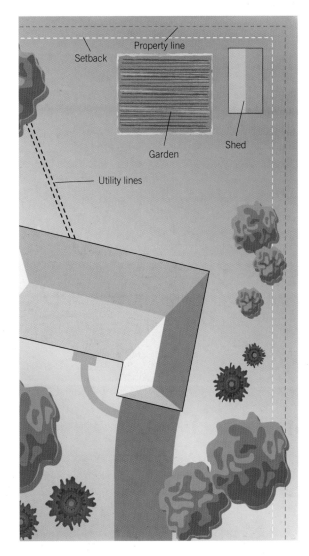

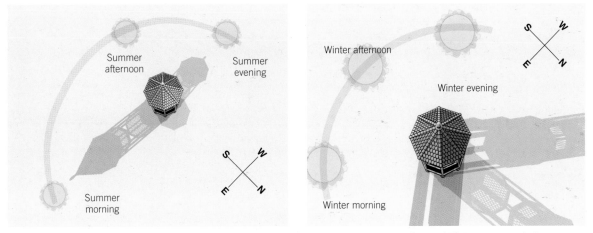

The effects of sunlight and shadow change throughout the year. Try to design window placements that maximize sun exposure in the winter and minimize it in the summer.

Topography

When assessing your property, note its topography—areas where the ground rises or dips. Avoid placing the shed at the bottom of a slope or in a low-lying area, where drainage is usually poor. A spot on a rise might be subject to high winds, which can cause damage and create a drafty, cold workspace. Avoid areas with soft, disturbed, or unstable soil as well; settling can cause the shed to warp or sag, preventing windows and doors from operating properly. Ideally, the site should be level.

Aesthetics

Practical considerations are important, but don't forget about aesthetics. How will the shed fit into the landscape? Do you want it at the end of a winding path or surrounded by a bed of flowers? Try to create a balance with the other features on the property—don't place it too close to other structures. Use your map to experiment with different configurations.

View

When choosing a site, stand in the spot you marked and look in all directions. Do you like the view? What will you see from the windows when you are working inside the shed? If you won't have windows in all four walls, design the shed so that the solid walls hide the least-favorable views. Consider whether you want to see the house from the shed and vice versa.

Look both ways before you make a siting choice. If your garden shed will have windows, make sure that what you see when you look out of them is appealing to you. And also consider how the windows themselves will look. These single-hung windows with multi-lite panes set an undeniable tone that is right at home with the character of this shed.

The strong Eastern design elements in this unusual garden shed are designed to complement the surrounding environment. The result is effective: the shed almost looks like it was grown in place rather than built.

BUILDING YOUR GARDEN SHED

You don't need to be a master carpenter to build a garden shed. A simple panelized kit can be assembled in a weekend (depending on the foundation) using standard tools and only a basic knowledge of carpentry. If your design is elaborate—with a complicated roofline, for example—or if you have no carpentry skills, you might want to hire a contractor for all or part of the job.

Materials

Any material used for building houses can be used for a shed. You can choose materials that match or complement your home, or you can seize the opportunity to use something different, such as those cedar shakes that you've always liked but found too expensive for a large project. Thanks to the variety of building materials available, you can customize any design to make it your own.

Sheet stock, (A) structural lumber, (B) and appearance-grade wood (C) all have a place in most shed plans.

Basic carpentry skills are required if you wish to build a successful shed from scratch. If you don't have much experience, you should definitely seek help from someone who does.

Framing, Siding & Roofing

Wood is the primary material used in building sheds. For structural members like wall studs and rafters, use construction-grade SPF (spruce, pine, or fir). While most houses are built with 2 × 4 or 2 × 6 wall studs, sheds normally can be built with lighter and slightly cheaper 2 × 3 studs, although only larger building centers and lumberyards stock 2 × 3. Rafters, beams, ridge poles, and floor joists typically are fashioned with 2 × 6 lumber. Floor joists, wood posts, and any wood shed parts that will be in contact with the ground must be made from pressure-treated lumber.

Plywood and Oriented Strand Board (OSB) are often used for roof and siding sheathing, and exterior-rated plywood may be used for siding and floors. Exterior-rated sheet stock, often with a textured finish or beading, can be used for siding that requires no backer panel of sheathing. Wood, in the forms of lap siding, shakes and other engineered products, is used for siding and roofing as well. Western red cedar is popular because of its natural resistance to insects and decay, as well as its visual appeal. Pine, fir, and hemlock are also good choices, provided that you plan to paint the shed. Other siding options include log-cabin siding, board-and-batten siding, and fiber-cementboard siding.

Roofing materials are often not included in shed kits, so you can choose standard or scalloped cedar or asphalt shingles, brightly colored corrugated metal, slate, clay tile, or even copper. If you use a heavy material on the roof, such as clay tile or slate, be sure that the framing and foundation will support the weight.

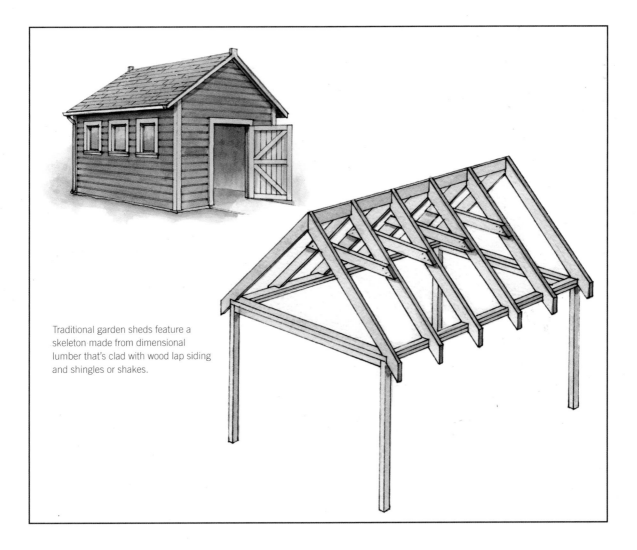

Traditional garden sheds feature a skeleton made from dimensional lumber that's clad with wood lap siding and shingles or shakes.

Foundation

A shed's foundation carries with it many of the demands of a greenhouse foundation, but primarily it must be level, provide adequate support and protect the structure from damage due to frost heave. The foundation may be as basic as a layer of compacted gravel or as complex as a concrete wall with a stucco or masonry finish. If you live in an area with freezing winters, you might want to construct a permanent foundation. Check with your planning department—local building codes may prescribe a particular foundation type. Before laying any foundation, be sure the layout is square and that you install utility lines if necessary. Some foundations are easier to build than others; consider whether you want to hire a professional.

Stacked Blocks

Concrete-block foundations are common for sheds, especially if the site is uneven or on a slope. They are sturdier than paving blocks or beams and are not quite as labor-intensive to install: Simply dig holes large enough to accommodate the blocks, fill the bottom with gravel, and stack the blocks on top, using construction adhesive to hold them together; then fill the remaining space in the holes with more gravel. Be sure the holes are deep enough to meet local building code requirements. If you plan to attach the shed to the blocks, fill the top blocks with concrete and insert anchor bolts into it before it sets.

Timbers can be leveled on a well-drained base to create a shed foundation. Drive rebar stakes through the timbers and into the ground to hold them in place.

Landscape blocks or pavers can be bonded together with construction adhesive and stacked on a well-drained, sturdy base to create a raised foundation for building a shed.

Wood posts set in concrete offer many possibilities for creating a foundation. Here, the floor joists are mounted directly to the sides of the posts with lag screws.

Wood Timbers

If your site is fairly level and you want to be able to move your garden shed in the future, you can attach the floor support system to a foundation of pressure-treated landscape timbers laid on a gravel bed (for drainage). Installing the gravel bed is labor-intensive, however—before laying the gravel, you'll need to excavate an area that's slightly larger than the footprint of the shed and as deep as is required by local building codes—usually 6" (15 cm).

Concrete

If you plan to use the shed only for storing garden tools, you may not think it needs a permanent foundation. However, a concrete-post, -footing, or -slab foundation is a good idea if you plan to use the shed year-round or for a larger structure, such as an office or a studio. In fact, local building codes might require a permanent foundation for structures of a certain size. To install concrete posts, dig holes that meet local codes, add gravel, and set tube forms into the holes. Fill the forms with concrete, and insert an anchor bolt or post bracket into the concrete (be sure the bracket is level) before it sets.

Although they are the sturdiest and most stable foundations, concrete footings and slabs are much more labor-intensive to build, so you might want to hire a contractor or use an existing concrete slab on your property. A concrete-slab foundation is recommended if you want to install plumbing or a heated floor or if you plan to store heavy items (such as a lawn tractor or large shop equipment) or pool equipment, which is wet and can rot a wood floor.

Other foundation options include suspending a floor undercarriage frame from wood posts that are set into concrete (inset), or pouring a concrete slab (above). A concrete slab is an excellent choice if you'll be parking lawn tractors or other vehicles in the shed—especially if a skirt is included to function as a driveway.

Windows & Doors

If you've ever considered making your own windows or doors, a shed is a perfect guinea pig of a structure. Fabricating fixed windows from wood frame stock and clear acrylic is about as cheap a way to obtain shed windows as you'll find. And you'd be surprised what a lovely door you can create from plain dimensional lumber or even sheet stock. Or, you can go the traditional route with your shed and simply buy windows and prehung doors that you like. A basic sash window (often called a barn sash) is very inexpensive.

Shed kits usually include windows and doors in myriad sizes and shapes, including octagonal windows and French-style divided lite windows, as well as picture windows, transoms, fan arches, and more. Fixed and operable models in hinged, sash, sliding and casement styles are available. Some suppliers offer only single glazing; others supply insulated glass. Window frame materials include wood, aluminum, vinyl and vinyl-clad wood. Kits often include window boxes and shutters, and some suppliers provide screens.

Door options include wood, steel, and fiberglass, with or without windows and screens. They can be single or double, in French, Dutch, or sliding styles. You can also choose to include a door lock or a hasp and padlock.

Kit sheds usually come with prehung doors and windows that are easy to install; they are typically major elements of the shed design.

Building and installing windows and doors yourself is a great way to save money and make sure you get exactly what you need. The clerestory windows in this shed are simply pieces of clear acrylic captured by wood stops. The door is made by framing pieces of exterior siding with strips of cedar.

Exterior Details

You can have fun creating a unique exterior with architectural details such as weathervanes, cupolas, finials, gingerbread trim, decorative shutters and windows, dormers, and window boxes. Scalloped shingles and copper panels add design flair, and even the hardware you choose for the door hinges and handles can impart character. Consider adding a porch, complete with a couple of comfy deck chairs for relaxing and taking in the view from your shed.

The tapered roofline and multilite doors on this fancy garden shed are set off perfectly by one simple design touch: the cupola with ball finial.

Shed Kits

Some suppliers offer a seemingly endless variety of options, including window and door styles, siding materials and colors, roof designs, and architectural details. Keep in mind that selecting more options can drive up the price and increase the time it takes for the supplier to gather the kit components before shipping. Roofing materials are not usually included in kits. Some manufacturers, especially those that offer cedar sheds, might include cedar shingles or shakes with their kits, but most leave the choice of roofing materials up to you.

Shipping is typically not included in the shed price. Wood is heavy, so shipping costs can be considerable. Don't forget to include them in your budget.

Be sure to ask the supplier exactly what the kit includes, and find out if a customer assistance line is available. Assembly instructions should be clear and comprehensive and include additional instructions for the options you have chosen. A good kit supplier will even provide an assembly video. As soon as the kit arrives, check that all of the materials and hardware are included before you begin any assembly.

Metal shed kits normally include the walls, roof and door but not the floor. You can usually buy a floor kit that goes with the sheds, or you can create your own floor and buy a manufacturer's kit for anchoring the shed with cables or spikes.

Panelized kits are a good cost compromise between building completely from scratch and hiring the whole job out. They are fairly easy to assemble but they do require the ability to follow directions and pay attention to detail. But with a little work, this explosion of walls will become the lovely shed seen within.

Many kit sheds feature walls that are fabricated from plastics or metal, although kits made from premium wood panels are also very popular. The kit shed above has plastic walls and door, metal wall studs, and a traditional asphalt shingle roof.

Kit Types

If you have even rudimentary carpentry skills, you can build a shed from a kit. Online suppliers offer a variety of options, plans, and kits in three general formats: precut, panelized (or pre-assembled), and prebuilt. Many suppliers also provide plans of their shed designs so you can build them yourself.

In a precut kit, the supplier has already cut the framing and siding and assembled the windows and doors. This option will save you money because you do almost all the assembly yourself. However, it takes more time than a pre-assembled kit, where the walls, floor, and trusses, as well as the doors and windows, arrive pre-assembled. All you have to do is put the panels together, attach the trusses, and add the roof sheathing and shingles. With basic carpentry skills and tools, you and a few friends can build this type of kit in a day or two (depending on your foundation). This type of kit will cost more than a precut kit.

The most expensive option is a prebuilt shed: You choose the style and options to customize it; the supplier builds it and delivers it your site.

Hardware kits, including structural gussets and lumber connectors, allow you to build a shed without having to make tricky cuts or calculate angles.

GARDEN SHED INTERIORS

A basic storage shed needn't look like an *Architectural Digest* layout, but it shouldn't be a dangerous mess. Hooks and storage shelves or cabinets encourage you to keep items organized, making them easier to find when you need them. If you plan to spend time in the shed, make it cozy and inviting by painting the walls or adding paneling and even rugs and throws. You can spruce up a shed with almost anything you'd use to decorate your home, so feel free to experiment!

White and apple-green paint brighten up the interior of this cheery little shed. And even if your garden shed isn't actually used for gardening, a gardening motif is always a good design strategy for a shed.

The beauty of sheds is that you don't have to treat them like feature projects in a lifestyle magazine. If a mélange of shelves, benches, pots, and simple tools suits your aesthetic, then you really do need a shed in your life.

A simple, sturdy floor like this plywood one can be dressed up with a throw rug for special occasions. Don't install carpeting, though—wall-to-wall carpet is perhaps the worst floorcovering you could put in a shed.

Floors

Shed kits typically include a plywood floor; for a more finished appearance, you can lay cedar, pine, or other wood floorboards over the plywood floor. The type of flooring you choose will depend on the elements and how you'll use the shed: A woodworking shop floor must withstand more abuse than the floor of a home office.

No matter what type of shed you build, flooring should be practical, durable, and easy to clean. Tile, stone, paving stones, and even linoleum are good choices, but avoid carpeting, which can become mildewed. (Instead, add throw rugs that can be removed and washed when necessary.) A potting shed floor might be made of gravel (which provides good drainage and acts as a heat sink), stone, or brick. If you have a concrete-slab foundation, you can add visual interest by tinting the concrete and embossing a pattern or texture.

Easy-to-clean surfaces like these mortared brick pavers make as much sense in a garden shed as they do in a greenhouse. This product works best when set into a sand or gravel base with no subfloor.

Walls

A weathered wooden shed can add character to a garden; to preserve its rustic charm, you might want to leave the shed's interior walls untouched, especially if they are cedar. If you've insulated the shed, you'll want to finish the interior walls with wood paneling or drywall and paint. Earthy colors are a good match for a garden shed, but a coat of white paint, even on bare wood walls, can transform an interior from dark and dingy to bright and airy. You can also stencil around the windows and doors or express your creativity with paint and decorative flourishes.

Storage

Organizational aids, such as hooks, shelving, and basic storage cabinets, are all available from home-improvement centers. A potting shed will also need a potting bench (see opposite) as well as plastic bins for soil and containers for storing small tools, pencils, tags, gloves, and other gardening paraphernalia. Scour flea markets and the recesses of your basement and garage for items you can recycle into storage containers. Repurposing items adds charm and keeps them out of the landfill.

Electricity, Heat, & Water

A home office or woodworking shop needs electricity and heat, and a crafts or art studio might also need plumbing. Even a humble potting shed will benefit from lighting and a nearby water source. The shed's location will have an impact on access to utilities. Running utility lines from the house to the shed will involve digging a trench. Use UF cable for electricity, and lay it to a depth prescribed by code. Remember to install conduit and plumbing before you lay the foundation. See pages 44 for more ideas about utilities and garden structures. And see pages 152 to 155 to learn how to supply water to your shed.

Heat

If you plan to use the shed year-round, you'll need to keep it warm. Begin by insulating the walls and ceiling just as you would a house and installing insulated windows; then add weather stripping around the windows and door. The most convenient heat source is an electric heater, although a wood stove or gas fireplace is also an option. If the shed faces south, you will gain the benefit of solar heat during the day. Tile or stone floors will store the heat and radiate it back into the room later in the day. You can also consider installing a heated floor, although it can be expensive.

Turn on the new circuit and test all of the receptacles and fixtures. Depress the Test button and then the Reset button if you installed a GFCI receptacle. If any of the fixtures or receptacles is not getting power, check the connections first and then test the receptacle or switch for continuity with a multimeter.

The Potting Bench

Even if you don't have a potting shed, a potting bench is a useful addition to any yard. Usually attached to a fence, shed, or wall in a sheltered spot, a bench offers plenty of space to repot indoor plants, seed flats of vegetables or flowers, or mix up soil without having to worry about getting dirt all over the floor. It's also a good place to store gardening tools and keep bins of soil handy. (To learn how to build a potting bench, see pages 130 to 135).

These two potting benches can be built against a wall inside your shed, or even against a fence near your garden. A good potting bench has some storage capacity as well as a sturdy worksurface.

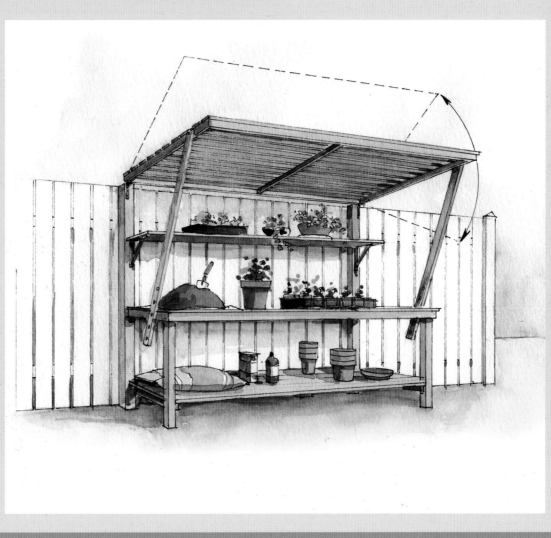

CHAPTER THREE

Greenhouse & Garden Shed Projects

ONE OF THE JOYS OF OWNING YOUR OWN GARDEN GETAWAY structure is customizing the space to meet your specific needs and preferences. In the same way that many woodworkers spend most of their workshop time improving on and adding to their space, many gardeners enjoy tinkering away in their shed or greenhouse, making it their own.

The projects featured on the following pages cover a range of customizations related to garden sheds. Some, such as building a brand new kit greenhouse yourself, are very ambitious. Others, such as making a cold frame or garden tote, take just a few hours and can be easily done by gardeners whose carpentry skills may not measure up to their cultivating skills.

Several projects in this chapter, such as the potting table and the garden bench, are necessary furnishings for any greenhouse or garden shed. By building these essentials you'll save money—money that's better spent on your real passion: plants, of course.

HARD-SIDED KIT GREENHOUSE

Building a greenhouse from a prefabricated kit offers many advantages. Kits are usually very easy to assemble because all parts are prefabricated and the lightweight materials are easy to handle. The quality of kit greenhouses varies widely, though, and buying from a reputable manufacturer will help ensure that you get many years of service from your greenhouse.

If you live in a snowy climate, you may need to either provide extra support within the greenhouse or be ready to remove snow whenever there is a significant snowfall because the lightweight aluminum frame members can easily bend under a heavy load. Before buying a kit, make sure to check on how snowfall may affect it.

Kit greenhouses are offered by many different manufacturers, and the exact assembly technique you use will depend on the specifics of your kit. Make sure you read the printed instructions carefully, as they may vary slightly from this project.

The kit we're demonstrating here is made from aluminum frame pieces and transparent polycarbonate panels and is designed to be installed over a base of gravel about 5" thick. Other kits may have different base requirements.

When you purchase your kit, make sure to uncrate it and examine all the parts before you begin. Make sure all the pieces are there and that there are no damaged panels or bent frame members.

A perfectly flat and level base is crucial to any kit greenhouse, so make sure to work carefully. Try to do the work on a dry day with no wind, as the panels and frame pieces can be hard to manage on a windy day. Never try to build a kit greenhouse by yourself. At least one helper is mandatory, and you'll do even better with two or three.

Construction of a kit greenhouse consists of four basic steps: laying the base, assembling the frame, assembling the windows and doors, and attaching the panels.

Kit greenhouses come in a wide range of shapes, sizes and quality. The best ones have tempered-glass glazing and are rather expensive. The one at right is glazed with corrugated polyethylene and is at the low end of the cost spectrum.

The familiar gambrel profile is tricky to create from scratch, but when purchased as a kit a gambrel greenhouse is a snap to assemble.

Some greenhouse kits include only the hardware necessary to create the frame structure. The glazing, which is normally some variety of plastic sheeting, is acquired separately.

Kit greenhouses (and other types, too) can be built in groups so you may create a variety of growing climates. This lets you raise species that may not have compatible needs for light, moisture and heat.

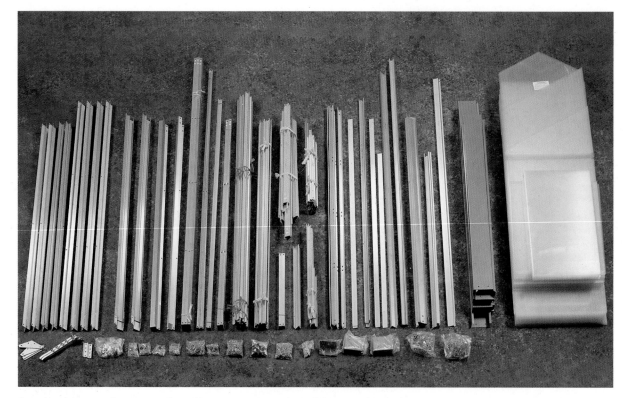

Organize and inspect the contents of your kit cartons to make sure all of the parts are present and in good condition. Most manuals will have a checklist. Staging the parts makes for a more efficient assembly. Just be sure not to leave any small parts loose, and do not store parts in high-traffic areas.

A cordless drill/driver with a nut-driver accessory will trim hours off of your assembly time compared with using only hand tools.

Rent outdoor power equipment if you need to do significant regrading to create a flat, level building base. Be sure to have your local utility company inspect for any buried utility lines first. (You may prefer to hire a landscaping company to do re-grading work for you.)

HOW TO Build a Kit Greenhouse

1 Create an outline for the base of the greenhouse using stakes and string. The excavation should be about 2" wider and longer than the overall dimensions of your greenhouse. To ensure that the excavation is perfectly square, measure the diagonals of the outline. If diagonals are equal, the outline is perfectly square. If not, reposition the stakes until the outline is square.

2 Excavate the base area to a depth of 5". Use a long 2 x 4 and a 4-ft. level to periodically check the excavation and make sure it is level and flat. You can also use a laser level for this job.

3 Assemble the base of the greenhouse, using the provided corner connectors and end connectors, attaching them with base nuts and bolts. Lower the base into the excavation area, and check to make sure it's level. Measure the diagonals to see if they are equal; if not, reposition the base until the diagonals are equal, which ensures that the base is perfectly square. Pour a layer of gravel or other fill material into the excavation, to within about 1" of the top lip of the base frame. Smooth the fill with a long 2 x 4.

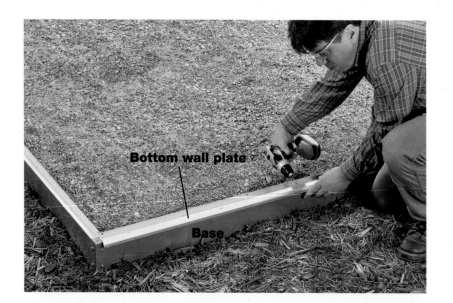

4 Attach the bottom wall plates to the base pieces so that the flanged edges face outside the greenhouse. In most systems, the floor plates will interlock with one another, end to end, with built-in brackets.

5 Fasten the four corner studs to the bottom wall plates, using hold-down connectors and bolts. In this system, each corner stud is secured with two connectors.

6 Assemble the pieces for each side ceiling plate, then attach one assembled side plate against the inside of the two corners studs, making sure the gutter is positioned correctly. Now attach the front ceiling plate to the outside of the two corner studs that are over the front floor plate.

7 Attach the other side ceiling plate along the other side, flat against the inside of the corner studs. Then attach corner brackets to the rear studs, and construct the back top plate by attaching the rear braces to the corners and joining the braces together with stud connectors.

8 Fasten the left and right rear studs to the outside of the rear floor plate, making sure the top ends are sloping upward, toward the peak of the greenhouse. Attach the center rear studs to the rear floor plate, fastening them to the stud connectors used to join the rear braces.

9 Attach the side studs on each side wall, using the provided nuts and bolts. Then attach the doorway studs to the front wall of the greenhouse.

10 Attach diagonal struts, as specified by the manufacturer. Periodically take diagonal measurements between the top corners of the greenhouse, adjusting as necessary so that the measurements are equal and the greenhouse square.

11 Fasten the gable-end stud extensions to the front and back walls of the greenhouse. The top ends of the studs should angle upward, toward the peak of the greenhouse.

Rafter

Crown

Crown Beam

12 Assemble the roof frame on a flat area near the wall assembly. First assemble the crown-beam pieces; then attach the rafters to the crown, one by one. The end rafters, called the crown beams, have a different configuration, so make sure not to confuse them.

13 With at least one helper, lift the roof into place onto the wall frames. The gable end studs should meet the outside edges of the crown beams, and the ends of the crown beams rest on the outer edge of the corner bracket. Fasten in place with the provided nuts and bolts.

Side Braces

Roof Support Window

14 Attach the side braces and the roof-window support beams to the underside of the roof rafters, as specified by the manufacturer's instructions.

Backwards and Forwards

With some kits you need to go backward to go forward. Because the individual parts of your kit depend upon one another for support, you may be required to tack all the parts together with bolts first and then undo and remake individual connections as you go before you can finalize them. For example, in this kit you must undo the track/brace connections one at a time so you can insert the bolt heads for the stud connectors into the track.

15 Build the roof windows by first connecting the two side window frames to the top window frame. Slide the window panel into the frame; then secure it by attaching the bottom window frame. Slide the window into the slot at the top of the roof crown; then gradually lower it in place. Attach the window stop to the window support beam.

16 Assemble the doors, making sure the top slider/roller bar and the bottom slider bar are correctly positioned. Lift the door panels up into place onto the top and bottom wall plates.

17 Install the panels one-by-one, using panel clips. Begin with the large wall panels. Position each panel and secure it by snapping a clip into the frame, at the intervals specified by the manufacturer's instructions.

18 Add the upper panels. At the gable ends, the upper panels will be supported by panel connectors that allow the top panel to be supported by the bottom panel. The lower panels should be installed already.

19 Install the roof panels and roof-window panels so that the top edges fit up under the edge of the crown or window support and the bottom edges align over the gutters.

20 Test the operation of the doors and roof windows and make sure they operate smoothly.

BUILD-IT-YOURSELF HOOPHOUSE

The hoophouse is a popular garden structure for two main reasons: it is cheap to build and easy to build. In many agricultural areas you will see hoophouses snaking across vast fields of seedlings, protecting the delicate plants at their most vulnerable stages. Because they are portable and easy to disassemble, they can be removed when the plants are established and less vulnerable.

While hoophouses are not intended as inexpensive substitutes for real greenhouses, they do serve an important agricultural purpose. And building your own is a fun project that the whole family can enjoy.

The hoophouse shown here is essentially a Quonset-style frame of bent ¾" PVC tubing draped with sheet plastic. Each semicircular frame is actually made from two 10-ft. lengths of tubing that fit into a plastic fitting at the apex of the curve. PVC tubes tend to stay together simply by friction-fitting into the fittings, so you don't normally need to solvent glue the connections (this is important to the easy-to-disassemble and store feature). If you experience problems with the frame connections separating, try cutting 4" to 6"-long pieces of ½" (outside diameter) PVC tubing and inserting them into the tubes and fittings like splines. This will stiffen the connections.

A hoophouse is a temporary agricultural structure designed to be low-cost and portable. Also called Quonset houses and tunnel houses, hoophouses provide shelter and shade (depending on the film you use) and protection from wind and the elements. They will boost heat during the day, but are less efficient than paneled greenhouses for extending the growing season.

TIP Building a Hoophouse

- ◇ Space frame hoops about 3 ft. apart.

- ◇ Leave ridge members a fraction of an inch (not more than ¼") shorter than the span, which will cause the structure to be slightly shorter on top than at the base. This helps stabilize the structure.

- ◇ Orient the structure so the wall faces into the prevailing wind rather than the end openings.

- ◇ If you are using long-lasting greenhouse fabric for the cover, protect the investment by spray-painting the frame hoops with primer so there is no plastic-to-plastic contact.

- ◇ Because hoophouses are temporary structures that are designed to be disassembled or moved regularly, you do not need to include a base.

- ◇ The ¾" PVC pipes used to make the hoop frames are sold in 10 ft. lengths. Two pipes fitted into a Tee or cross fitting at the top will result in legs that are 10 ft. apart at the base and a ridge that is roughly 7 ft. tall.

- ◇ Clip the hoophouse covers to the end frames. Clips fastened at the intermediate hoops will either fly off or tear the plastic cover in windy conditions.

Row tunnels are often used in vegetable gardens to protect sensitive plants in the spring and fall. Plastic or fabric sheeting is draped over short wire or plastic framework to protect plants at night. During the heat of the day, the sheeting can be drawn back to allow plants direct sunlight.

Hoophouse frames can be made from wood instead of PVC plastic. Wood allows you to attach plastic sheeting with retainer strips and staples.

Building & Siting a Hoophouse

The fact that a hoophouse is a temporary structure doesn't give you license to skimp on the construction. When you consider how light the parts are and how many properties sheet plastic shares with boat sails, the importance of securely anchoring your hoophouse becomes obvious. Use long stakes (at least 24") to anchor the tubular frames, and make sure you have plenty of excess sheeting at the sides of the hoophouse so the cover can be held down with ballast. Creating pockets at the ends of the sheeting and inserting scrap lumber is the ballasting technique shown here, but it is also common (especially when building in a field) to weigh down the sheeting by burying the ends in dirt. Only attach the sheeting at the ends of the tubular frame, and where possible, orient the structure so the prevailing winds will blow through the tunnel.

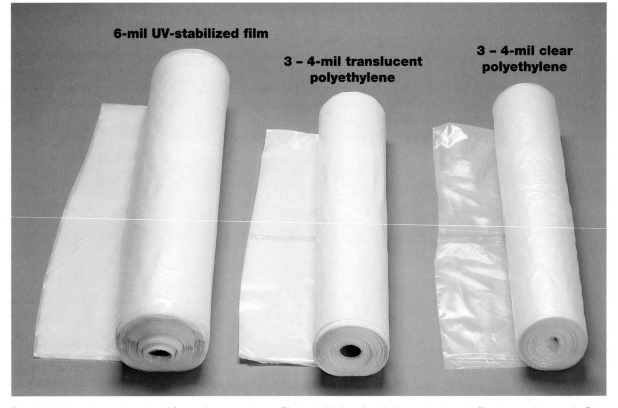

6-mil UV-stabilized film

3 – 4-mil translucent polyethylene

3 – 4-mil clear polyethylene

Sheet plastic is an inexpensive material for creating a greenhouse. Obviously, it is less durable than polycarbonate, fiberglass or glass panels. But UV-stabilized films at least 6-mil thick can be rated to withstand four years or more of exposure. Inexpensive polyethylene sheeting (the kind you find at hardware stores) will hold up for a year or two, but it becomes brittle when exposed to sunlight. Some greenhouse builders prefer to use clear plastic sheeting to maximize the sunlight penetration, but the cloudiness of translucent poly makes it effective for diffusing light and preventing overheating. For the highest quality film coverings, look for film rated for greenhouse and agricultural use.

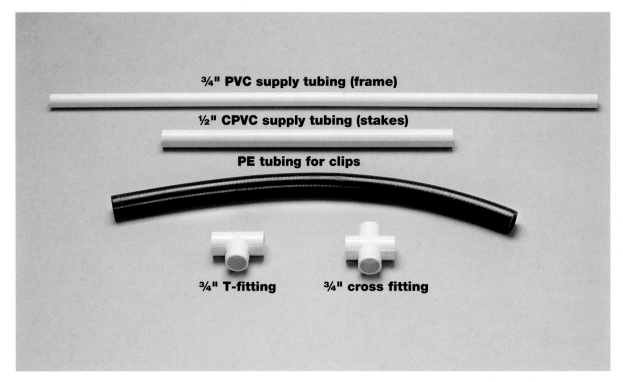

¾" PVC supply tubing (frame)

½" CPVC supply tubing (stakes)

PE tubing for clips

¾" T-fitting   **¾" cross fitting**

Plastic tubing and fittings used to build this hoophouse include: Light duty ¾" PVC tubing for the frame (do not use CPVC—it is too rigid and won't bend properly); ½" CPVC supply tubing for the frame stakes (rigidity is good here); Polyethylene (PE) tubing for the cover clips; T-fittings and cross fittings to join the frame members.

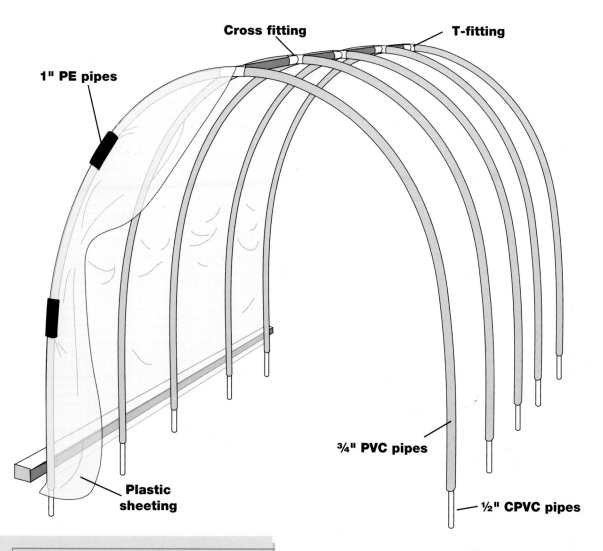

Cross fitting

T-fitting

1" PE pipes

Plastic sheeting

¾" PVC pipes

½" CPVC pipes

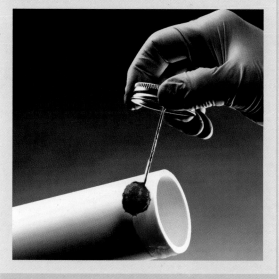

TIP Making it Permanent

Solvent-weld the pipes from the frame to the T-fitting and cross fittings if your hoophouse is intended to be a permanent fixture. If you may be disassembling and moving the structure, it's fine to rely on tension fittings with PVC pipe.

Tools and Materials

(for 10-ft. wide by 15-ft. long project seen here):

- (14) ¾" x 10 ft. PVC pipes
- (4) ½" x 10 ft. CPVC pipes
- (1) 1" x 10 ft. PE pipe (black)
- (4) ¾" PVC cross fittings
- (2) ¾" PVC T-fittings
- 20 ft. x 16 ft. clear or translucent plastic sheeting
- (4) 16-ft. Pressure-treated 2 x 4

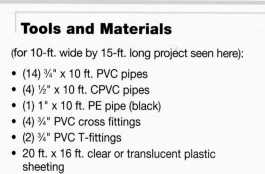

HOW TO Make a Build-It-Yourself Hoophouse

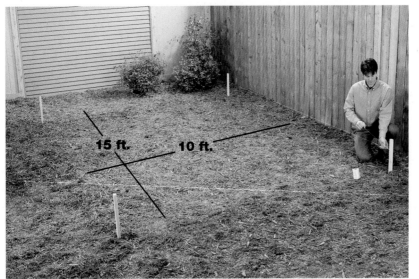

1 Lay out the installation area using stakes and mason's string. Strive for square corners, but keep in mind that these are relatively forgiving structures, so you can miss by a little bit and probably won't be able to notice.

15 ft.   10 ft.

2 Cut a 30"-long stake from ½" CPVC supply tubing for each leg of each hoop frame. Measure out from the corners of the layout and attach a piece of high-visibility tape on the string at 3-ft. intervals; then drive a stake at each location. When the stake is fully driven, 10" should be above ground and 20" below.

3 Join the two legs for each frame hoop with a fitting. Use a tee fitting for the end hoop frames and a cross fitting for the intermediate hoop frames. No priming or solvent gluing is necessary. (The friction-fit should be sufficient, but it helps if you tap on the end of the fitting with a mallet to seat it.)

4 Slip the open end of one hoop-frame leg over a corner stake so the pipe is flush against the ground. Then bend the pipes so you can fit the other leg end over the stake at the opposite corner. If you experience problems with the pipes pulling out of the top fitting, simply tape the joints temporarily until the structure frame is completed.

5 Continue adding hoop frames until you reach the other end of the structure. Wait until all the hoop frames are in place before you begin installing the ridge poles. Make sure the cross fittings on the intermediate hoop frames are aligned correctly to accept the ridge poles.

6 Add the ridge-pole sections between the hoop frames. Pound on the end of each new section as you install it to seat it fully into the fitting. Install all of the poles.

7 Cut four pieces of pressure-treated 2 x 4 to the length of the hoophouse (15 ft. as shown). Cut the roof cover material to size. (We used 6-mil polyethylene sheeting.) It should be several inches longer than is necessary in each direction. Tack the cover material at one end of the 2 x 4 and then continue tacking it as you work your way toward the end. Make sure the material stays taut and crease-free as you go.

8 Lay a second 2 x 4 the same length as the first over the tacked plastic so the ends and edges of the 2 x 4s are flush. Drive a 3" deck screw through the top 2 x 4 and into the lower one every 24" or so, sandwiching the cover material between the boards. Lay the assembly next to one edge of the hoophouse and pull the free end of the material over the tops of the frames.

9 On the other side of the structure, extend the cover material all the way down so it is taut and then position another 2 x 4 underneath the fabric where it meets the ground. Staple the plastic and then sandwich it with a final 2 x 4.

10 Make clips to secure the roof cover material from a 12"-long section of hose or soft tubing. Here, 1"-dia., thin-walled PE supply tubing is slit longitudinally and then slipped over the material to clip it to the end frames. Use at least six clips per end. Do not clip at the intermediate hoop frames.

OPTION: Make doors by clipping a piece of cover material to each end. (It's best to do this before attaching the main cover.) Then cut a slit down the center of the end material. You can tie or tape the door material to the sides when you want it open and weigh down the pieces with a board or brick to keep the door shut. This solution is low-tech but effective.

A-FRAME GREENHOUSE

A greenhouse can be a decorative and functional building that adds beauty to your property. A greenhouse also can be a quick-and-easy, temporary structure that serves a purpose and then disappears. The wood-framed greenhouse seen here fits somewhere between these two types. The sturdy wood construction will hold up for many seasons. The plastic sheeting covering will last one to four or five seasons, depending on the materials you choose (see page 108), and it is easy to replace when it starts to degrade.

The 5-ft.-high kneewalls in this design provide ample space for installing and working on a conventional-height potting table. The walls also provide some space for plants to grow. For a door, this plan simply employs a sheet of weighted plastic that can be tied out of the way for entry and exit. If you plan to go in and out of the greenhouse frequently, you can purchase a prefabricated greenhouse door from a greenhouse materials supplier. To allow for ventilation in hot weather, we built a wood-frame vent cover that fits over one rafter bay and can be propped open easily.

You can use hand-driven nails or pneumatic framing nails to assemble the frame if you wish, although deck screws make more sense for a small structure like this.

A wood-frame greenhouse with sheet-plastic cover is an inexpensive, semipermanent gardening structure that can be used as a potting area as well as a protective greenhouse.

Nothing beats the look of a wooden A-frame greenhouse. This kit greenhouse, set on a raised foundation and properly maintained, will provide decades of service while making a delightful aesthetic contribution to the garden.

This plastic door kit is secured in place with self-adhesive zipper strips, and can be rolled up for access or to create venting on hot days. Kits are available from greenhouse suppliers or you can make your own roll-up door with zipper strips and plastic purchased from a building center.

This aluminum-frame kit greenhouse is lightweight and easy to assemble. The aluminum structure will also hold up well to weather and will likely be more durable than wood-frame structures.

Cutting List: A-Frame Greenhouse

KEY	NO.	PART	DIMENSION	MATERIAL
A	2	Base ends	3-½" x 3-½" x 96"	4 x 4 landscape timber
B	2	Base sides	3-½" x 3-½" x 113"	4 x 4 landscape timber
C	2	Sole plates end	1-½" x 3-½" x 89"	2 x 4 pressure treated
D	2	Sole plates side	1-½" x 3-½" x 120"	2 x 4 pressure treated
E	12	Wall studs side	1-½" x 3-½" x 57"	2 x 4
F	1	Ridge support	1-½" x 3-½" x 91"	2 x 4
G	2	Back studs	1-½" x 3-½" x 76" *	2 x 4
H	2	Door frame sides	1-½" x 3-½" x 81" *	2 x 4
I	1	Cripple stud	1-½" x 3-½" x 16"	2 x 4
J	1	Door header	1-½" x 3-½" x 32"	2 x 4
K	2	Kneewall caps	1-½" x 3-½" x 120"	2 x 4
L	1	Ridge pole	1-½" x 3-½" x 120"	2 x 4
M	12	Rafters	1-½" x 3-½" x 60" *	2 x 4

Approximate dimension; take actual length and angle measurements on structure before cutting.

Materials

- (1) 20 x 50-ft. roll 4 or 6-mil polyethylene sheeting or greenhouse fabric, tack strips
- (12) 24"-long pieces of No. 3 rebar
- (4) 16-ft. pressure-treated 2 x 4
- (2) exterior-rated butt hinges
- (1) screw-eye latch
- (8) 8" timber screws

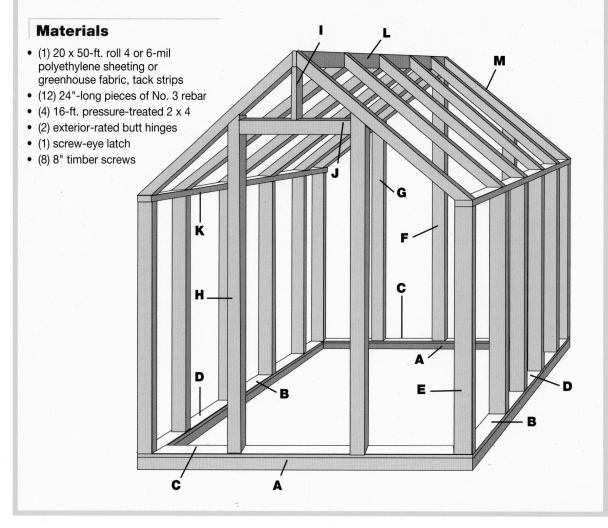

HOW TO Build an A-Frame Greenhouse

1 Prepare the installation area so it is flat and well drained (see page 99); then cut the base timbers (4 x 4 landscape timbers) to length. Arrange the timbers so they are flat and level and create a rectangle with square corners. Drive a pair of 8" timber screws at each corner, using a drill/driver with a nut-driver bit.

2 Cut 12 pieces of No. 3 rebar (find it in the concrete supplies section of any building center) to 24" in length to use as spikes for securing the timbers to the ground. A metal cutoff saw or a reciprocating saw with a bimetal blade can be used to make the cuts. Drill a ⅜" guide hole through each timber near each end and in the middle. Drive a rebar spike at each hole with a maul or sledge hammer until the top is flush with the wood.

3 Cut the plates and studs for the two side walls (called knee-walls). Arrange the parts on a flat surface and assemble the walls by driving three 3" deck screws through the cap and base plates and into the ends of the studs. Make both kneewalls.

4 Set the base plate of each kneewall on the timber base and attach the walls by driving 3" deck screws down through the base plates and into the timbers. For extra holding power you can apply exterior panel adhesive to the undersides of the plates, but only if you don't plan to relocate the structure later.

Temporary post

5 Cut the ridge support post to length and attach it to the center of one end base plate, forming a T. Cut another post the same length for the front (this will be a temporary post) and attach it to a plate. Fasten both plates to front and back end timbers.

Ridge pole

6 Set the ridge pole on top of the posts and check that it is level. Also check that the posts are level and plumb. Attach a 2 x 4 brace to the outer studs of the kneewalls and to the posts to hold them in square relationship. Double-check the pole and posts with the level.

7 Cut a 2 x 4 to about 66" to use as a rafter template. Hold the 2 x 4 against the end of the ridge pole and the top outside corner of a kneewall. Trace along the face of the ridge and the top plate of the wall to mark cutting lines. Cut the rafter and use it as a template for the other rafters on that side of the roof. Create a separate template for the other side of the roof.

8 Mark cutting lines for the rafters, using the templates and cut them all. You'll need to use a jigsaw or handsaw to make the bird's-mouth cuts on the rafter ends that rest on the kneewall.

9 Attach the rafters to the ridge pole and the kneewalls with deck screws driven through pilot holes. Try to make the rafters align with the kneewall studs.

10 Mark the positions for the remaining end wall studs on the base plate. At each location, hold a 2 x 4 on end on the base plate and make it level and plumb. Trace a cutting line at the top of the 2 x 4 where it meets the rafter. Cut the studs and install them by driving screws toenail-style.

11 Measure up 78" (or less if you want a shorter door) from the sole plate in the door opening and mark a cutting line on the temporary ridge post. Make a square cut along the line with a circular saw or cordless trim saw (inset). Then cut the door header to fit between the vertical door frame members. Screw the header to the cut end of the ridge post and drive screws through the frame members and into the header.

Tack strips

12 Begin covering the greenhouse with your choice of cover material. (We used 6-mil polyethylene sheeting.) Start at the ends. Cut the sheeting to size and then fasten it by attaching screen retainer strips to wood surfaces at the edges of the area being covered. Tack the sheeting first at the top, then at the sides and finally at the bottom. After the strips are installed (use wire brads), trim the sheeting along the edges of the strips with a utility knife.

13 Attach the sheeting to the outside edge of the base plate on one side. Roll sheeting over the roof and down the other side. Draw it taut and cut it slightly overlong with scissors. Attach retainer strips to the other base plate and then to the outside edges of the corner studs.

Door

2×4 weight

14 Make and hang a door. We simply cut a piece of sheet plastic a little bigger than the opening (32") and hung it with retainer strips from the header. Attach a piece of 2 x 4 to the bottom of the door for weight.

OPTION: Make a vent window. First, cut a hole in the roof in one rafter bay and tack the cut edges of the plastic to the faces (not the edges) of the rafters, ridge pole and wall cap. Then build a frame from 1 x 2 stock that will span from the ridge to the top of the kneewall and extend a couple of inches past the rafters at the side of the opening. Clad the frame with plastic sheeting and attach it to the ridge pole with butt hinges. Install a screw-eye latch to secure it at the bottom. Make and attach props if you wish.

GARDEN SHED WITH WINDOWS

This unique outbuilding is part greenhouse and part shed, making it perfect for a year-round garden space or backyard sunroom, or even an artist's studio. The front facade is dominated by windows—four 29 × 72" windows on the roof, plus four 29 × 18" windows on the front wall. When appointed as a greenhouse, two long planting tables inside the shed let you water and tend to plants without flooding the floor. If gardening isn't in your plans, you can omit the tables and cover the entire floor with plywood, or perhaps fill in between the floor timbers with pavers or stones.

Because sunlight plays a central role in this shed design, consider the location and orientation carefully. To avoid shadows from nearby structures, maintain a distance between the shed and the structure that's at least 2½ times the height of the obstruction. With all of that sunlight, the temperature inside the shed is another important consideration. You may want to install some roof vents to release hot air and water vapor.

Some other details that make this 10 × 12-ft. shed stand out are the homemade Dutch door, with top and bottom halves that you can open together or independently, and its traditional saltbox shape. The roof covering shown here consists of standard asphalt shingles, but cedar shingles make for a nice upgrade.

HOW TO Build a Garden Shed with Windows

1 Build the foundation, following the basic steps used for a wooden skid foundation (see page 117). First, prepare a bed of compacted gravel. Make sure the bed is flat and level. Cut seven 4 × 4" × 10-ft. pressure-treated posts down to 115¾" to serve as floor joists. Level each joist, and make sure all are level with one another and that the ends are flush. Add rim joists and blocking: Cut two 12-ft. 2 × 4s (142¾") for rim joists. Fasten the rim joists to the ends of the 4 × 4 joists with 16d galvanized common nails.

2 Cut ten 4 × 4 blocks to fit between the joists. Install six blocks 34½" from the front rim joist, and install four blocks 31½" from the rear. Toenail the blocks to the joists. All blocks, joists, and sills must be flush at the top.

3 To frame the rear wall, cut one top plate and one pressure-treated bottom plate (142¾"). Cut 12 studs 81". Assemble the wall. Raise the wall and fasten it to the rear rim joist and the intermediate joists, using 16d galvanized common nails. Brace the wall in position with 2 × 4 braces staked to the ground.

4 For the front wall, cut two top plates and one treated bottom plate (142¾"). Cut ten studs (35¾") and eight cripple studs (13¼"). Cut four 2 × 4 window sills (31¹¹⁄₁₆"). Assemble the wall. Add the double top plate, but do not install the window stops at this time. Raise, attach, and brace the front wall.

5 Cut lumber for the right side wall: one top plate (54⅞"), one treated bottom plate (111¾"), four studs (81"), and two header post studs (86⅞"); and for the left side wall: top plate (54⅞"), bottom plate (111¾"), three studs (81"), two jack studs (77½"), two posts (86⅞"), and a built-up 2 × 4 header (39¼"). Assemble and install the walls. Add the doubled top plates along the rear and side walls. Install treated 2 × 4 nailing cleats to the joists and blocking.

6 Trim two sheets of ¾" plywood as needed and install them over the joists and blocking, leaving open cavities along the front of the shed and a portion of the rear. Fasten the sheets with 8d galvanized common nails driven every 6" along the edges and 8" in the field. Fill the exposed foundation cavities with 4" of gravel and compact it thoroughly.

7 Construct the rafter header from two 2 × 8s cut to 142¾". Join the pieces with construction adhesive and pairs of 10d common nails driven every 24" on both sides. Set the header on top of the side wall posts, and toenail it to the posts with four 16d common nails at each end.

8 Cut pattern rafters to use as rafter templates. Test-fit the rafters. One should rest squarely on the rafter header, and its bottom end should sit flush with the outside of the front wall. Adjust the rafter cuts as needed; then use the pattern rafters to mark and cut the remaining rafters.

9 Cut the 2 × 6 ridge board (154¾"). Mark the rafter layout onto the ridge and front and rear wall plates. Install the rafters and ridge. Make sure the rafters are spaced accurately so the windows will fit properly into their frames.

10 Cut a short rafter, test-fit, and adjust as needed. Cut the remaining seven short rafters and install them. Measure and cut four 2 × 4 nailers (311⁄16") to fit between the sets of rafters. Position the nailers and toenail them to the rafters.

11 Complete the rake portions of each side wall. Mark the stud layouts on the bottom plate and on the top plate of the square wall section. Use a plumb bob to transfer the layout to the rafters. Measure for each stud, cutting the top ends of the studs under the rafters at 45° and at 30°. Toenail the studs to the plates and rafters. Add horizontal 2 × 4 nailers.

12 Create the inner and outer window stops from 10-ft.-long 2 × 4s. For stops at the sides and tops of the roof windows and all sides of the front wall windows, rip the inner stops to 2¼" wide and the outer stops to 1" wide. For the bottom of each roof window, rip the inner stop to 1½"; bevel the edge of the outer stop at 45°.

13 Install each window as follows: Attach inner stops as shown in the drawings, using galvanized finish nails. Paint or varnish the rafters and stops for moisture protection. Apply a heavy bead of caulk as shown. Set the glazing in place, add another bead of caulk, and attach the outer stops. Cover the rafters and stop edges with 1 × 4 trim.

14 Cover the walls with T1-11 siding, starting with the rear wall. Trim the sheets as needed so they extend from the bottom edges of the rafters down to at least 1" below the tops of the foundation timbers. On the side walls, add Z-flashing above the first row and continue the siding up to the rafters.

15 Install 1 × 6 fascia over the ends of the A rafters. Keep all fascia ½" above the rafters so it will be flush with the roof sheathing. Using scrap rafter material, cut the 2 × 4 lookouts (5¼"). On each outer B rafter, install one lookout at the bottom end and four more spaced 24" on center going up. On the A rafters, add a lookout at both ends and two spaced evenly in between. Install the 1 × 6 rake boards (fascia).

16 Rip 1 × 6 boards to 5¼" width (some may come milled to 5¼" already) for the gable soffits. Fasten the soffits to the lookouts with siding nails. Rip a 1 × 8 board for the soffit along the rear eave, beveling the edges at 30° to match the A rafter ends. Install the soffit.

17 Deck the roof with ½" plywood sheathing, starting at the bottom ends of the rafters. Install metal drip edge, building paper, and asphalt shingles following the steps. If desired, add one or more roof vents during the shingle installation. Be sure to overlap shingles onto the 1 × 4 trim board above the roof windows.

18 Construct the planting tables from 2 × 4 lumber and 1 × 6 boards. The bottom plates of the table legs should be flush with the outside edges of the foundation blocking.

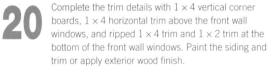

19 Build each of the two door panels using T1-11 siding, 2 × 2 bracing, a 2 × 4 bottom rail, and 1 × 2 trim on the front side. The panels are identical except for a 2 × 4 sill added to the top of the lower panel. Install 1 × 2 stops at the sides and top of the door opening. Hang the doors with four hinges, leaving even gaps all around. Install a bolt latch for locking the two panels together.

20 Complete the trim details with 1 × 4 vertical corner boards, 1 × 4 horizontal trim above the front wall windows, and ripped 1 × 4 trim and 1 × 2 trim at the bottom of the front wall windows. Paint the siding and trim or apply exterior wood finish.

COLD FRAME

A cold frame allows you to plant seeds six to eight weeks earlier in the season. Though a few plants reliably grow in soil temperatures of 40–50°F (4–10°C), virtually all do best when soil temperatures are above 60°F (16°C). Planting in warm soil avoids the risk of fungal diseases that can rot seeds or cause seedlings to fail soon after germination.

Install your cold frame over a base of fresh manure covered with a deep layer of topsoil. As the manure decomposes, it will warm the soil above it. The translucent top of the cold frame will capture heat from sunlight and protect the plants within.

Step 1: Assemble the Box

A. Cut the sides, front and back panels, and corner braces as indicated on the cutting list.

B. Assemble the box by screwing the side, front, and back panels to the front and back corner braces.

Step 2: Assemble the Cover

A. Cut a ¾"-deep kerf down the center of one long edge of each horizontal cover frame.

B. Drill pilot holes in the cover frame pieces and in the fiberglass panel. Fit the fiberglass into the kerfs and fasten it in place with wood screws.

C. Set the horizontal cover frame and panel on top of the vertical frame pieces. Fasten the frame at the corners, using three wood screws for each.

D. Fasten the fiberglass panel to the vertical frame pieces, using screws and washers.

Step 3: Attach the Cover

A. Attach the butt hinges to the inside of the cover, 8" from each back corner.

B. Position the cover and align it with the edges. Fasten the hinges to the back of the box.

Step 4: Install the Cold Frame

A. In a sunny, protected spot, dig a rectangular hole, 36 × 42 × 24" deep. Add a 10 to 12" layer of fresh manure or nitrogen-rich compost.

B. Line the hole with plastic; then fit the cold frame into it. Backfill soil securely around the frame.

C. Each spring, remove the cold frame, dig down, and add a new layer of manure or compost.

This simple cold frame is a sloping plywood box with a light-filtered corrugated panel for a top.

HOW TO Build a Cold Frame

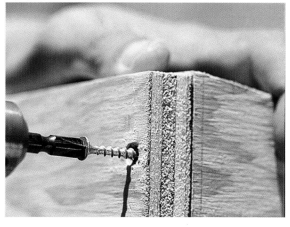

1 Assemble the box and use wood screws to fasten the pieces.

2 Fasten the fiberglass panel into kerfs cut in the horizontal cover frame; then assemble the cover.

3 Attach the hinges to the inside of the frame cover and then to the back panel of the box. Add interior corner braces (optional).

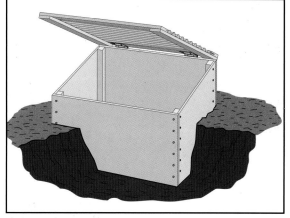

4 Dig a hole, add a layer of compost, and install the cold frame.

Cutting List: Cold Frame

NO.	PART	DIM.	MATERIAL
1	Back panel	26 × 36"	¾" plywood
1	Front panel	22 × 36"	¾" plywood
2	Side panels	22 × 26 × 28½"	¾" plywood
2	Vertical cover frames	5½ × 30"	¾" plywood
2	Horizontal cover frames	4 × 36"	¾" plywood
2	Back corner braces	26"	2 × 2"

Tools and Materials:

- (2) exterior-rated butt hinges
- Circular saw
- Drill
- Shovel
- Plastic liner
- 4 × 8 ft. × ¾" CDX plywood panel
- 26 × 36" corrugated fiberglass panel
- 8-ft. 2 × 2" treated lumber
- ¼ × 1¼" corrosion-resistant wood screws
- (12) ½" × ⅛" corrosion resistant washers

POTTING TABLE

If you are like many gardeners, your equipment expands into all available space—basement, garage, tool shed, closets, and spare rooms. A potting table can help you get organized by providing a convenient spot to store tools and materials during the off-season. Then, when the garden comes alive, you can move the potting table outdoors and use it to transplant seedlings, clean containers, mix fertilizer, and perform other messy tasks.

This potting table is broad enough to hold several pots and trays of nursery starts. Its open shelving is useful for storing materials, and the pegboards give you a great place to hang trowels, forks, and dibbles—in or out of season.

We chose to leave this potting bench unpainted and unfinished, but if you'd prefer to finish it, by all means do so. Just be sure to use exterior rated finishing materials and if you are painting make sure to use a paint with an enamel finish. You'll find it much easier to clean the semi-gloss or flat paint. If you do not anticipate moving the potting bench omit the casters.

The potting table or bench is the backbone of most greenhouses and garden sheds. Here is a simple one that can be made with everyday materials.

Cutting List: Potting Table

Pressure-Treated Lumber:			
NO.	PART	DIM.	LENGTH
4	Legs	2 × 6	30"
2	Top crossbraces	2 × 6	31"
2	Lower crossbraces	2 × 6	32½"
4	Crossbrace blocks	2 × 6	12"
4	Caster-mount blocks	2 × 6	5½"
6	Work-surface planks	2 × 6	72"
2	Work-surface supports	2 × 6	31"
4	Lower-shelf planks	2 × 6	66"

Lumber			
NO.	PART	DIM	LENGTH
1	Front apron support	2 × 4	52"
1	Front apron	1 × 6	66"
2	Side aprons	1 × 6	22"
3	Vertical supports	2 × 8	18"
1	Top shelf	1 × 8	72"
1	Middle shelf	1 × 8	34⅛"
Pegboard Pressboard Sheet ⅜" (10 mm):			
1	Top shelf backing	22 × 72"	

Tools and Materials

- Caster assemblies with wheel locks and fasteners
- Pegboard hooks, vinyl-covered hanger hooks
- Pressure-treated lumber
- ⅛" and ¼" drill bits
- Circular saw
- Power drill
- Clamps
- Socket wrench
- Pegboard
- Corrosion-resistant deck screws
- Hex bolts
- Nuts and washers
- Exterior wood glue
- Wood preservative
- Tape measure
- Framing square

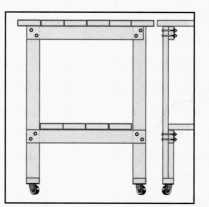

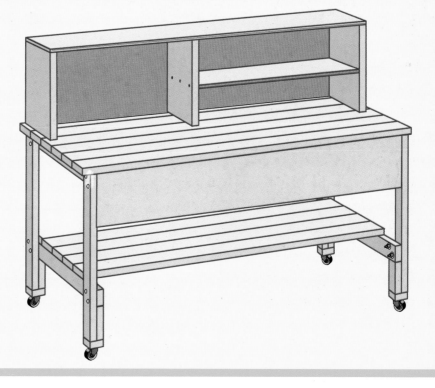

HOW TO Build A Potting Table

1 Attach the crossbrace blocks to the ends of the legs, using deck screws; then attach the top and bottom crossbraces between the legs, using bolts and washers.

2 Glue together the planks of the work surface and let them dry. Attach the work-surface supports and the apron supports, using deck screws.

3 Drill pilot holes and attach a leg assembly to each end of the work surface assembly. Add a caster to the bottom of each leg.

4 Cut four shelf planks; rip one plank to be 5" wide. Position the planks between the lower crossbraces and attach them, using deck screws.

Step 1: Build the Leg Assemblies

A. Cut the legs, crossbraces, crossbrace blocks, and caster-mount blocks to size, following the cutting list on page 131. On a flat work surface, position a crossbrace block on each leg, flush with the sides and bottom edge of the leg. Drill pilot holes and attach the crossbrace blocks with glue and four deck screws for each leg.

B. Align the legs, parallel with one another and 33" apart. Set the lower crossbrace in place, the long edge tight to the crossbrace blocks and the ends flush with the outside edge of each leg. Place the upper crossbrace flush with the top corners of the front and back legs, allowing a 1½" setback from the front leg edge. Square up the assembly and clamp it in place; mark and drill two ¼" holes at each leg-crossbrace junction.

C. Thread a washer onto each bolt; then drive the bolts through the legs and crossbraces. Attach the final washer and nut on each bolt; then tighten them just until the wood compresses. Release the clamps as each joint is secured.

D. Align a caster block at the foot of each leg and attach each with four deck screws.

E. Repeat steps 1 – 4 for the second leg assembly.

Step 2: Assemble the Work Surface

A. Cut the work-surface planks, work-surface supports, and front apron support. Loosely align the six planks, squaring them into a rectangle. Apply glue to each edge of the four central planks; then square and clamp them tightly and allow to dry overnight.

B. Measure 4½" in and draw a line across each end of the assembly. Position a work surface support inside each line, flush with the assembly's back edge and 2" short of its front edge; clamp together.

C. Drill ⅛ × 2" pilot holes, two in each plank, through the support and into—but not through—the planks. Attach the supports to the assembly with deck screws.

D. Drill pilot holes and attach the front apron support between the work-surface supports, using deck screws.

Step 3: Attach the Legs

A. Place the work-surface assembly facedown on a level surface. Position a leg assembly on each end, aligning each flush with the back edge, parallel to and snug against a work surface support.

B. Drill ⅛" pilot holes horizontally through the top crossbrace into a work-surface support and fasten the leg assembly with deck screws. Repeat for the other leg assembly.

C. Drill pilot holes and install a caster assembly on the caster-mount block on the bottom of each leg. Use the hardware supplied with the casters to secure them.

Step 4: Add the Bottom Shelf

A. Cut four bottom-shelf planks. Using a circular saw, rip a plank to 5" wide.

B. Stand the potting bench on its legs, check that it is square, and then place the bottom-shelf planks so they span the bottom crossbraces. Align each plank with the outer edge of the crossbraces; clamp in place and drill two ⅛" pilot holes through each plank end into the crossbrace. Fasten with deck screws.

TIP Choosing Lumber

If you are planning to leave your potting table unfinished, build it with wood that resists damage from moisture. Cedar and redwood are two wood species that are naturally resistant and each would make a fine potting table. A more economical choice is pressure-treated pine. In the past, many gardeners have been reluctant to use treated lumber because the treating agent contained chromated copper arsenate (CCA), which is classified as a hazardous material. Today, however, CCA has been replaced by several less toxic alternatives, including copper azole, ACQ and borate. Consequently, there is no reason to avoid treated lumber when making garden accessories.

Step 5: Install the Shelf Unit

A. Cut the vertical shelf supports, top, and middle shelf; cut the pegboard backing.

B. On two shelf supports, mark a line 8½" from an end. Set the supports and the middle shelf on a flat surface, with the middle shelf between the two shelf supports and lined up with the marks. Drill pilot holes through the supports and into the shelf, then attach the shelf; with deck screws.

C. Add the upper shelf and the remaining shelf support, laying them out so the ends of the top shelf are flush with the sides of the shelf supports. Drill three pilot holes for each support and attach the shelf with deck screws.

D. Align the pegboard with the shelf assembly; the lower edge of the pegboard should extend 4" beyond the ends of the shelf supports. Fasten the pegboard to the shelf supports, using deck screws.

Step 6: Add the Aprons & Shelf Unit

A. Cut the side and front aprons. Fit the side aprons flush against the upper crossbraces, using the crossbraces as a stop. Drill pilot holes through the aprons and fasten them with deck screws.

B. Fit the front apron onto the apron support, drill pilot holes, and fasten the apron, using deck screws.

Step 7: Install Hooks & Accessories

A. Position the shelf unit on top of the work surface and align the sides. Mark the locations of the shelf supports on the work surface, remove the shelf, and drill pilot holes through the work surface, two to each support.

B. Set the shelf unit back in place. Working from the underside, attach the shelf unit to the work surface with deck screws. Fasten the overhanging edge of the pegboard to the work surface, using deck screws.

C. Apply a coat of wood preservative to the entire assembly.

D. Hang hooks from the pegboard. Drill equally spaced ¼" pilot holes across the aprons and attach vinyl hooks for hand tools. If desired, attach wire baskets to the lower shelf unit.

5 Assemble the shelves and shelf supports, then attach the pegboard to the back of this upper shelf unit.

6 Attach the side aprons to the upper crossbraces and the front apron to the apron support. Secure the shelf unit to the top of the work surface.

7 Attach the sides and back of the shelf unit to the work surface. Install hooks and add accessories.

Container Gardening

Planting in permanent containers requires care to ensure good results. First, picking the right container is a practical decision as well as a decorative one. You can use everything from a half-barrel to a wicker basket—the only requirement is that your pot or container have adequate drainage and be waterproof.

Inexpensive plastic pots are excellent for retaining water; set them inside more attractive containers if you wish, or dress them up by planting trailing annuals to cover the sides. Unglazed terra cotta pots are quite porous, allowing soil to breathe and plant roots to cool; they're a good choice for plants that require thorough drainage. Overcome the need for frequent watering in terra cotta by painting the insides with waterproof latex sealant. Still other options are glazed clay pots and thick wooden planters, both of which hold moisture better than unglazed pottery.

PLANTER BOXES

Decorating a garden is much like decorating a room in your home—it's nice to have pieces that are adaptable enough that you can move them around occasionally and create a completely new look. After all, most of us can't buy new furniture every time we get tired of the way our living rooms look. And we can't build or buy new garden furnishings every time we want to rearrange the garden.

That's one of the reasons this trio of planter boxes works so well. In addition to being handsome —especially when flowers are bursting out of them—they're incredibly adaptable. You can follow these plans to build a terrific trio of planter boxes that will go well with each other and will complement most gardens, patios, and decks. Or you can tailor the plans to suit your needs. For instance, you may want three boxes that are exactly the same size. Or you might want to build several more and use them as a border that encloses a patio or frames a terraced area.

Whatever the dimensions of the boxes, the basic construction steps are the same. If you decide to alter the designs, take a little time to figure out the new dimensions and sketch plans. Then devise a new cutting list and do some planning so you can make efficient use of materials. To save cutting time, clamp together parts that are the same size and shape and cut them as a group (called gang cutting).

When your planter boxes have worn out their welcome in one spot, you can easily move them to another, perhaps with a fresh coat of stain and add new plantings. You can even use the taller boxes to showcase outdoor relief sculptures—a kind of alfresco sculpture gallery.

Whether you build only one or all three, these handy cedar planters are small enough to move around your gardens and inside your greenhouse or garden shed.

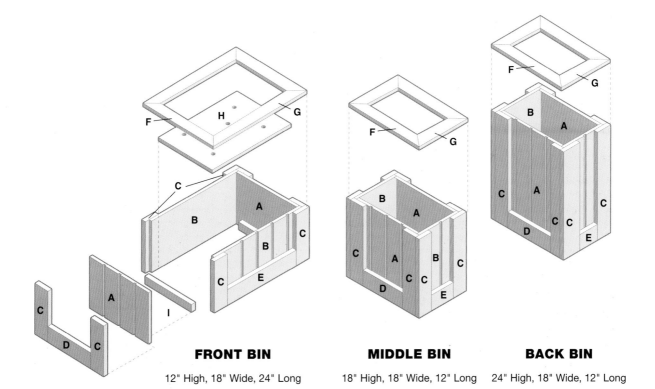

FRONT BIN

12" High, 18" Wide, 24" Long

MIDDLE BIN

18" High, 18" Wide, 12" Long

BACK BIN

24" High, 18" Wide, 12" Long

Cutting List: Planter Box

KEY	NO.	PART	FRONT BIN DIMENSION	MIDDLE BIN DIMENSION	BACK BIN DIMENSION	MATERIAL
A	2	End panel	⅝ × 15 × 11⅛"	⅝ × 15 × 17⅛"	⅝ × 15 × 23⅛"	Siding
B	2	Side panel	⅝ × 22¼ × 11⅛"	⅝ × 10¼ × 17⅛"	⅝ × 10¼ × 23⅛"	Siding
C	8	Corner trim	⅞ × 3½ × 11⅛"	⅞ × 3½ × 17⅛"	⅞ × 3½ × 23⅛"	Cedar
D	2	Bottom trim	⅞ × 3½ × 9¼"	⅞ × 3½ × 9¼"	⅞ × 3½ × 9¼"	Cedar
E	2	Bottom trim	⅞ × 3½ × 17"	⅞ × 3½ × 5"	⅞ × 3½ × 5"	Cedar
F	2	Top cap	⅞ × 1½ × 18"	⅞ × 1½ × 18"	⅞ × 1½ × 18"	Cedar
G	2	Top cap	⅞ × 1½ × 24"	⅞ × 1½ × 12"	⅞ × 1½ × 12"	Cedar
H	1	Bottom panel	¾ × 14½ × 19½"	¾ × 14½ × 8½"	¾ × 14½ × 8½"	Plywood
I	2	Cleat	⅞ × 1½ × 12"	⅞ × 1½ × 12"	⅞ × 1½ × 12"	Cedar

Note: Measurements reflect the actual size of dimension lumber.

Tools and Materials

- Tape measure
- Circular saw
- Straightedge
- Drill
- Finishing sander
- Miter box and backsaw
- (3) 8-ft. cedar 1 × 2s
- (6) 8-ft. cedar 1 × 4s

- 4 × 8-ft. sheet of ⅝" T1-11 siding
- 2 × 4-ft. piece ¾" CDX plywood
- 1¼" galvanized deck screws
- 1½" galvanized deck screws
- 6d galvanized finish nails
- Exterior wood stain
- Paintbrush

HOW TO Build Planter Boxes

Step 1: Make & Assemble the Box Panels

A. Following the cutting list on page 137, cut the end panels (A) and side panels (B), using a circular saw and a straightedge cutting guide (photo 1).

B. Put one end panel facedown on your work surface, butting it up against the side panel, face-side-out. Mark positions and drill several counterbored 3⁄32" pilot holes in the side panel.

C. Fasten the side panel to the end panel with 1½" deck screws. Repeat this process to fasten a second side panel to the end panel.

D. Put the remaining end panel facedown on the work surface. Take the assembled pieces and place the open end over the second end panel, side panels flush with the end-panel edges. Drill counterbored pilot holes in the side panels, and attach the side panels to the end panel, using deck screws.

Step 2: Attach the Trim

A. Cut the corner trim (C) to length. Overlap the edges of the corner trim pieces at the corner, forming a square butt joint. Fasten the corner trim pieces to the panels by driving 1¼" deck screws through the inside faces of the panels and into the corner pieces (photo 2).

B. To provide extra support, drive screws or galvanized finish nails through the overlapping corner trim pieces and into the edges of the adjacent trim piece.

C. Cut the bottom trim pieces (D, E) to length. Fasten them to the end and side panels, between the corner-trim pieces. Drive 1¼" deck screws through the side and end panels and into the bottom trim pieces.

D. Cut the top caps (F, G) to length. Cut 45° miters at both ends of one cap piece, using a miter box and backsaw.

E. Tack the mitered cap piece to the top edge of the planter, with the outside edges flush with the outer edges of the corner-trim pieces. For a proper fit, use this cap piece to guide the marking and cutting of the miters on the other cap pieces.

F. Miter both ends of each piece. Tack it to the box so it makes a square corner with the previously installed piece. If the corners don't fit just right, loosen the pieces and adjust them until everything is square.

G. Permanently attach all of the cap pieces to the box, using 6d galvanized finish nails.

Step 3: Install the Box Bottom & Apply Finish.

A. Cut the cleats (I) to length, and screw them to the end panels with 1½" deck screws (photo 3). On taller planters, it's best to mount the cleats higher on the panels so you won't need as much soil to fill the box—a savings in cost and weight. In that case, add cleats on the side panels for extra support.

B. Cut the bottom panel (H) to size from ¾"-thick CDX plywood. Drill several 1"-diameter weep holes in this panel. Set the panel onto the cleats—it does not need to be fastened in place.

C. Using a finishing sander, remove rough spots and splinters from all edges and surfaces. Apply two or three coats of exterior wood stain to all surfaces, and let the planter dry.

1 Cut the end panels and side panels to size.

2 Drive screws through the inside faces of the panels to fasten the corner-trim pieces.

3 Cut the cleats to length and screw them to the end panels.

Planter Boxes

- To help keep planter boxes from becoming discolored, line them with landscape fabric before adding soil. Simply cut a piece of fabric large enough to wrap the box as if you were gift-wrapping it, and then fold it to fit inside the box. Staple the fabric at the top of the box and trim off the excess. Add a 2" layer of gravel, and then add potting soil and plants.

- If your yard or garden is partially shaded, you may want to add wheels or casters to your planter boxes so you can move them to follow the sun. Casters also make it easier to bring the planters indoors during cold weather. Be sure to use locking wheels or casters with brass or plastic housings.

- If you're not experienced at arranging color combinations, start with a simple approach. Stay within the basic hot (red, yellow, and orange) or cool (blue, purple, and green) color families to create visual harmony.

  You can plant a collection of flowers and foliage in your favorite color, or try combining a variety of hues of the same color. If you want to add contrast, add some plants in neutral tones.

- Proportion, or the size and scale of plants in relationship to one another and the container, is another important component of successful plantings.

  In general, plant tall plants in large containers and low-lying plants in smaller ones. To achieve balance, use a dominant plant to establish a focal point, and then fill in around it with a combination of colors, textures, and shapes.

- Before purchasing plants for any container, consider their preferred growing conditions. Grouping plants with similar soil, watering, and fertilization requirements simplifies your work during the growing season.

INDOOR/OUTDOOR GARDEN BENCH

Casual seating is a welcome addition to any outdoor setting. It is a great way to enjoy a beautiful landscape. This lovely garden bench sits neatly at the borders of any porch patio or deck. It creates a pleasant resting spot for up to three adults without taking up a lot of space.

The straightforward design of this bench lends itself to accessorizing. Station a rustic cedar planter next to the bench for a lovely effect, or add a framed lattice trellis to one side of the bench to filter out wind and direct sunlight.

This bench design can be built using dimensional lumber that does not require any milling. Just cut it to length. Be sure to account for the actual dimension of the stock however: for example, a 1 × 4 is actually ¾ × 3½". Once you've finished, you can apply a clear sealant with UV protection, or let the wood mellow into a muted gray as it oxidizes.

No shed or greenhouse is complete without a good sturdy garden bench. Here is a plan for one that can be built with everyday lumber using everyday tools.

Cutting List: Garden Bench

KEY	NO.	PART	DIM.	MAT.
A	4	Leg half	1½ × 7¼ × 14½"	Cedar
B	8	Cleat	¾ × 3½ × 16"	Cedar
C	3	Brace	1½ × 1½ × 16"	Cedar
D	1	Trestle	1½ × 3½ × 60"	Cedar
E	2	Apron	1½ × 5½ × 60"	Cedar
F	8	Slat	1½ × 1½ × 60"	Cedar

Note: Measurements reflect the actual size of dimension lumber.

Tools and Materials

- (1) 2 × 8"× 6' cedar
- (4) 2 × 2" × 10' cedar
- (1) 2 × 4" × 6' cedar
- (1) 2 × 2" × 6' cedar
- (1) 1 × 4" × 12' cedar
- Moisture-resistant glue
- Wood sealer or stain
- 1½" and 2½" deck screws

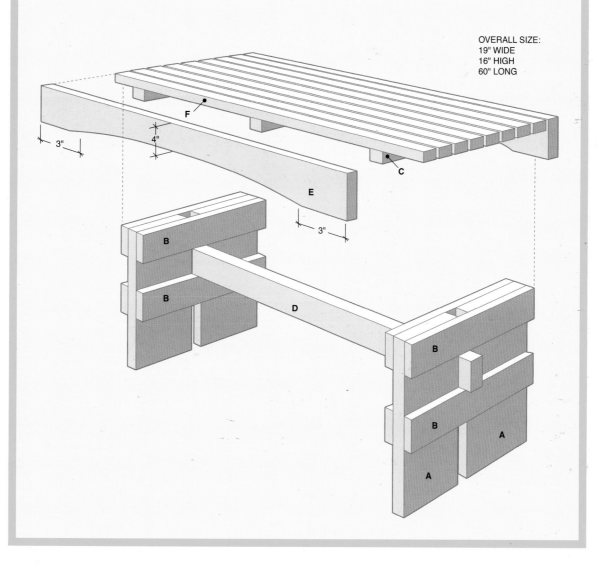

OVERALL SIZE:
19" WIDE
16" HIGH
60" LONG

HOW TO Build A Garden Bench

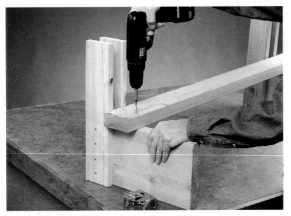

1 Make sure the trestle is positioned correctly against the cleats, and attach it to the leg.

2 Attach the remaining leg half to the cleats on both ends to complete the leg assembly.

3 Attach the outer brace for the seat slats directly to the inside faces of the cleats.

4 Use a flexible ruler pinned between casing nails to trace a smooth arch on the aprons.

5 Attach a 2 × 2 slat to the top inside edge of each apron, using 2½" deck screws and glue.

6 Attach the seat slats with glue and 1½" deck screws. Insert ½"-thick spacers to set gaps between the slats.

Step 1: Build the Base

A. Cut the leg halves (A), cleats (B) and trestle (D) to length. Sandwich one leg half between two cleats so the cleats are flush with the top and the outside edge of the leg half. Then join the parts by driving four 1½" deck screws through each cleat and into the leg half. Assemble two more cleats with a leg half in the same fashion.

B. Stand the two assemblies on their sides, with the open ends of the cleats pointing upward. Arrange the assemblies so they are roughly 4' apart. Set the trestle onto the inner edges of the leg halves, pressed flush against the bottoms of the cleats. Adjust the position of the assemblies so the trestle overhangs the leg half by 1½" at each end. Fasten the trestle to each leg half with glue and 2½" deck screws (photo 1).

C. Attach another pair of cleats to each leg half directly below the first pair, positioned so each cleat is snug against the bottom of the trestle.

D. Slide the other leg half between the cleats, keeping the top edge flush with the upper cleats. Join the leg halves with the cleats using glue and 2½" deck screws (photo 2).

E. Cut the braces (C) to length. Fasten one brace to the inner top cleat on each leg assembly, so the tops are flush (photo 3).

Step 2: Make the Aprons

A. Cut the aprons (E) to length. Prepare to lay out the arch on one apron, starting 3" from each end. The peak of the arch, located over the midpoint of the apron, should be 1½" up from the bottom edge.

B. Create a smooth, even arch by driving a casing nail at the peak of the arch and one at each of the starting points. Slip a flexible ruler behind the nails at the starting points and in front of the nail at the peak to create a smooth arch. Then trace along the inside of the ruler to make a cutting line (photo 4).

C. Cut along the line with a jigsaw and sand smooth.

D. Trace the profile of the arch onto the other apron and make and sand the cut.

E. Cut the slats (F) to length. Attach a slat to the top inside edge of each apron with glue and deck screws (photo 5).

Step 3: Install the Aprons and Slats

A. Apply glue at each end on the bottom sides of the attached slats. Flip the leg and trestle assembly and position it flush with the aprons so that it rests on the glue on the bottoms of the two slats. The aprons should extend 1½" beyond the legs at each end of the bench. Drive 2½" deck screws through the braces and into both slats.

B. Position the middle brace (C) between the aprons, centered end-to-end on the project. Fasten it to the two side slats with deck screws.

C. Position the six remaining slats on the braces, using ½"-thick spacers to create equal gaps between them. Attach the slats with glue and drive 2½" deck screws up through the braces and into each slat (photo 6).

Step 4: Apply Finishing Touches

A. Sand the slats smooth with progressively finer sandpaper. Wipe away the sanding residue with a rag dipped in mineral spirits. Let the bench dry. Apply a finish of your choice—a clear wood sealer protects the cedar without altering the color.

TIP Countersink Screws and Leveling Furniture

When sinking galvanized deck screws, use a counterbore bit or a standard ⅜"-dia. bit to drill ¼"-deep counterbores, centered on ⅛"-dia. pilot holes.

One trick for leveling furniture is to set a plastic wading pool on a flat plywood surface that is set to an exact level position with shims. Fill the pool with about ¼" of water. Set the furniture in the pool; then remove it quickly. Mark the tops of the waterlines on the legs, and use them as cutting lines for trimming the legs to level.

GARDEN TOTE

This compact carrying tote has plenty of room and is ideal for gardeners. With special compartments sized for seed packages, spray cans and hand tools, it is a quick-and-easy way to keep your most-needed supplies organized and ready to go. The bottom shelf is well suited to storing kneeling pads or towels. The gentle curves in the sides of the storage compartment allow easy access and provide a decorative touch. The sturdy cedar handle has a comfortable hand-grip cutout. Whether you're tending a small flower patch or a sprawling vegetable garden, you'll find this tote to be an indispensable gardening companion.

This lovely cedar garden tote can be used to move your most-used tools from shed to greenhouse to garden and back again. It's a snap to build.

Cutting List: Garden Tote

KEY	NO.	PART	DIM.	MAT.
A	2	Ends	$\frac{7}{8}$ × 9¼ × 11"	Cedar
B	2	Sides	$\frac{7}{8}$ × 5½ × 18"	Cedar
C	2	Shelves	$\frac{7}{8}$ × 9½ × 18"	Cedar
D	1	Divider	$\frac{7}{8}$ × 3½ × 16¼"	Cedar
E	2	Post	$\frac{7}{8}$ × 1½ × 14"	Cedar
F	1	Handle	$\frac{7}{8}$ × 1½ × 16¼"	Cedar
G	2	Partition	$\frac{7}{8}$ × 3½ × 3$\frac{7}{8}$"	Cedar

Note: Measurements reflect the actual size of dimension lumber.

Tools and Materials

- (1) 1 × 10" × 6' cedar
  (1) 1 × 6" × 6' cedar
  (1) 1 × 4" × 6' cedar
  (1) 1 × 2" × 6' cedar
- Moisture-resistant glue
- 1½ and 2" deck screws
- Finishing materials

OVERALL SIZE:
18⅝" HIGH
11" WIDE
19¾" LONG

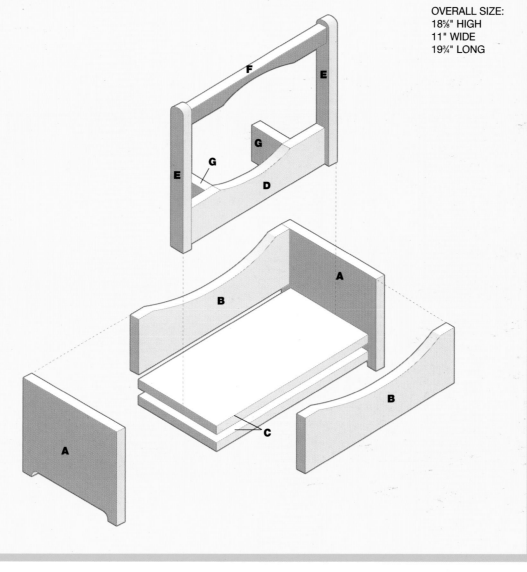

HOW TO Build a Garden Tote

Step 1: Build the Box

The gardener's tote has curved cutouts to improve access and scalloped ends to create feet. All screws are counterbored to ¼" depth for a smooth appearance. A counterbore bit will help you avoid drilling too deep.

A. Cut the ends (A), sides (B) and shelves (C) to size. Sand all parts smooth with medium-grit sandpaper.

B. On one side, mark points on one long edge, 1½" in and 1½" down. Draw a graceful curve between the points to form the cutting. Cut the curve with a jigsaw and sand it smooth.

C. Position the sides so the edges and ends are flush. Then trace the curve onto the uncut side and cut it to match. Clamp the sides together, and gang-sand both curves smooth.

D. Use a compass to draw ¾"-radius semicircles on the bottom edge of the end pieces, with centerpoints 1¾" from each end.

E. Using a straightedge, draw a line connecting the tops of the semicircles to complete the cutout shape. Cut the curves with a jigsaw (photo 1) and sand the ends smooth.

F. To attach the end and side pieces, drill ⅛" pilot holes at each end, ⁷⁄₁₆" in from the edges. Position the pilot holes 1", 3" and 5" down from the tops of the ends. Counterbore the holes.

G. Apply glue to the ends of the side pieces—making sure the top and outside edges are flush—and fasten them to the end pieces with 2" deck screws, driven through the end pieces and into the side pieces.

H. Mark the shelf locations on the inside faces of the ends. The bottom of the lower shelf is ¾" up from the bottoms of the ends, and the bottom of the upper shelf is 3¾" up from the bottoms of the ends.

I. Drill pilot holes ⁷⁄₁₆" up from the lines. Apply glue to the shelf ends, and position the shelves flush with the lines marked on the end pieces. Drive 2" deck screws through the pilot holes in the end pieces and into the shelves (photo 2).

Step 2: Build the Divider Assembly

The divider and partitions are assembled first, and then inserted into the box.

A. Cut the divider (D), posts (E), handle (F) and partitions (G) to size.

B. Draw a ⅜"-radius semicircle, using a compass, to mark the cutting line for a roundover at one end of each post. Use a sander to make the roundover.

C. The divider and handle have shallow arcs cut on one long edge. To draw the arcs, mark points 4" from each end. Then, mark a centerpoint ⅝" in from one long edge on the handle. On the divider, mark a centerpoint ⅝" from one long edge.

D. Draw a graceful curve to connect the points, and cut along the lines with a jigsaw. Sand the parts smooth.

E. Drill two pilot holes on each end of the divider, ⁷⁄₁₆" out from the start of the curve. Counterbore the holes. Attach the divider to the partitions, using glue and 2" deck screws driven through the divider and into the edges of the partitions.

F. To mark the positions of the divider ends, clamp the posts together with their edges flush, and mark a 3½"-long reference line on each post, ⅞" from the meeting point between the two posts. Start the reference lines at the square post ends. Connect the lines at the tops to indicate the position of the divider ends.

G. Drill two pilot holes through the posts, centered between each reference line and the inside edge. Counterbore the holes (photo 3). Drill and counterbore two more pilot holes in each post, centered ½" and 1" down from the tops.

H. Position the handle and divider between the posts, aligned with the pilot holes. One face of the divider should be flush with a post edge. Fasten the handle and divider between the posts with moisture-resistant glue and 2" deck screws, driven through the post holes. Set the assembly in the box. Make sure the partitions fit square with the side.

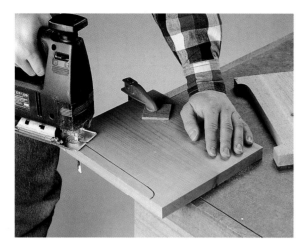

1 Use a jigsaw to cut the curves on the bottom edge of each end, forming feet for the box.

2 Attach the shelves by driving deck screws through the end pieces and into the ends of the shelves.

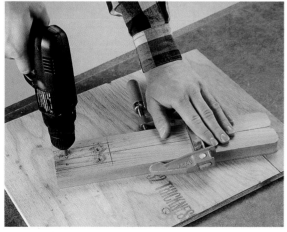

3 Drill and counterbore pilot holes in the posts before you attach them to the handle and divider.

Step 3: Install the Divider Assembly

A. Trace position lines for the posts on the end pieces (photo 4). Apply glue where the posts will be fastened. Drill pilot holes through the posts and counterbore the holes. Then attach the posts with 1¼" deck screws, driven through the pilot holes and into the ends.

B. Drill two evenly spaced pilot holes in the side adjacent to the partitions. Counterbore the holes; then drive 2" deck screws through the holes and into the edges of the partitions.

Step 4: Apply the Finishing Touches

A. Sand all surfaces smooth with medium (100- or 120-grit) sandpaper. Then finish-sand with fine (150- or 180-grit) sandpaper. Apply exterior wood stain to all surfaces if you want to preserve the cedar tones. Or for a more rustic appearance you can leave the wood uncoated, and the tote will slowly turn gray.

> **TIP Colder Climates**
>
> Many seed types, soil additives and other common gardening supplies should not be stored outdoors in subfreezing temperatures. If you live in a colder climate, load up your tote with these items in the fall, and store the tote in a warm spot for the winter.

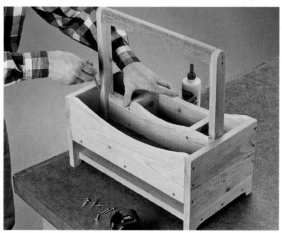

4 Draw reference lines for the post position on the box ends.

TRELLIS PLANTER

The decorative trellis and the cedar planter are two staples found in many yards and gardens. By integrating the appealing shape and pattern of the trellis with the rustic, functional design of the cedar planter, this project showcases the best qualities of both furnishings.

Because the 2 × 2 lattice trellis is attached to the planter, not permanently fastened to a wall or railing, the trellis planter can be moved easily to follow changing sunlight patterns or to occupy featured areas of your yard. It is also easy to move into storage during the winter. You may even want to consider installing wheels or casters on the base for greater mobility.

Building the trellis planter is a very simple job. The trellis portion is made entirely of strips of 2 × 2 cedar, fashioned together in a crosshatch pattern. The planter bin is a basic wood box, with panel sides and a two-board bottom with drainage holes that rests on a scalloped base. The trellis is screwed permanently to the back of the planter bin.

Stocking the trellis planter is a matter of personal taste and growing conditions. In most areas, ivy, clematis and grapevines are good examples of climbing plants that can be trained up the trellis. Ask at your local gardening center for advice on plantings. You can set containers of plants in the bin or fill the bin with potting soil and then add plants.

Tools and Materials

- (1) 2 × 6" × 8' cedar
- (1) 2 × 4" × 6' cedar
- (4) 2 × 2" × 8' cedar
- (3) 1 × 6" × 8' cedar
- (1) 1 × 2" × 6' cedar
- Moisture-resistant glue
- #8 2" wood screws
- 1⅝" and 2½" deck screws
- Finishing materials.

Cutting List: Trellis Planter

KEY	NO.	PART	DIMENSION	MAT.
A	12	Box slats	⅞ × 5½ × 13"	Cedar
B	2	Base front and back	1½ × 5½ × 25"	Cedar
C	2	Base ends	1½ × 5½ × 12¾"	Cedar
D	1	Cap front	1½ × 3½ × 25"	Cedar
E	2	Cap ends	1½ × 3½ × 14¼"	Cedar
F	1	Cap back	1½ × 1½ × 18"	Cedar
G	2	End posts	1½ × 1½ × 59½"	Cedar

KEY	NO.	PART	DIMENSION	MAT.
H	1	Center post	1½ × 1½ × 63½"	Cedar
I	1	Long rail	1½ × 1½ × 30"	Cedar
J	3	Medium rails	1½ × 1½ × 24"	Cedar
K	2	Short rails	1½ × 1½ × 18"	Cedar
L	2	Long cleats	⅞ × 1½ × 18½"	Cedar
M	2	Short cleats	⅞ × 1½ × 11"	Cedar
N	2	Bottom boards	⅞ × 5½ × 20¼"	Cedar

Note: Measurements reflect the actual size of dimension lumber.

OVERALL SIZE:
69" HIGH
17¼" DEEP
30" LONG

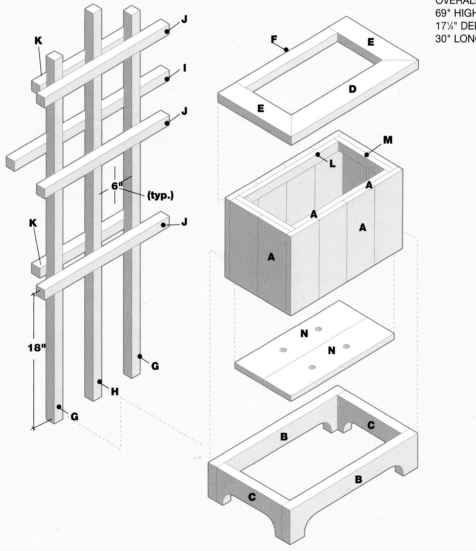

HOW TO Build a Trellis Planter

 Attach the side cleats flush with the tops of the side boards.

2 The recess beneath the bottom boards in the planter bin provides access for driving screws.

3 Before attaching the cap ends, drill pilot holes through the mitered ends of the cap-front ends.

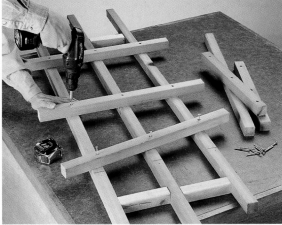

4 Temporary spacers hold the posts in position while the rails are attached.

Step 1: Build the Planter Bin

A. Cut the box slats (A) and cleats (L, M) to length. Arrange the slats edge-to-edge in two groups of four and two groups of two, with tops and bottoms flush.

B. Center a long cleat (L) at the top of each set of four slats, so the distance from each end of the cleat to the end of the panel is the same. Attach the cleats to the four-slat panels by driving 1⅝" deck screws (photo 1) through the cleats and into the slats.

C. Lay the short cleats (M) at the tops of the two-slat panels. Attach them to the slats the same way.

D. Arrange all four panels into a box shape and apply moisture-resistant wood glue to the joints. Attach the panels by driving 1⅝" deck screws through the four-slat panels and into the ends of the two-slat panels.

Step 2: Install the Bin Bottom

A. Cut the bottom boards (N) to length. Set the bin upside down on your work surface, and mark reference lines on the inside faces of the panels, ⅞" in from the bottom of the bin. Insert the bottom boards into the bin, aligned with the reference lines to create a ⅞" recess. Scraps of 1× cedar can be put beneath the bottom boards as spacers.

B. Drill ⅛" pilot holes through the panels. Counterbore the holes slightly with a counterbore bit. Fasten the bottom boards by driving 1⅝" deck screws through the panels and into the edges and ends of the bottom boards.

Step 3: Build the Planter Base

A. The planter base is scalloped to create feet at the corners.

B. Cut the base front and back (B) and the base ends (C) to length. To draw the contours for the scallops on the front and back boards, set the point of a compass at the bottom edge of the base front, 5" in from one end. Set the compass to a 2½" radius and draw a curve to mark the curved end of the cutout. Draw a straight line to connect the tops of the curves, 2½" up from the bottom of the board, to complete the scalloped cutout.

C. Make the cutout with a jigsaw, then sand any rough spots. Use the board as a template for marking a matching cutout on the base back.

D. Draw a similar cutout on one base end, except with the point of the compass 3½" in from the ends. Cut out both end pieces with a jigsaw.

E. Draw reference lines for wood screws ¾" from the ends of the base front and back. Drill three evenly spaced pilot holes through the lines. Counter-bore the holes. Fasten the base ends between the base front and back by driving three evenly spaced deck screws at each joint.

Step 4: Attach the Bin to the Base

A. Set the base frame and planter bin on their backs. Position the planter bin inside the base so it extends ⅞" past the top of the base.

B. Drive 1⅝" deck screws through the planter bin and into the base to secure the parts (photo 2).

Step 5: Make the Cap Frame

A. Cut the cap front (D), cap ends (E) and cap back (F) to length. Cut 45° miters at one end of each cap end and at both ends of the cap front.

B. Join the mitered corners by drilling pilot holes through the joints (photo 3). Counterbore the holes. Fasten the pieces with glue and 2½" deck screws. Clamp the cap front and cap ends to the front of your worktable to hold them while you drive the screws.

C. Fasten the cap back between the cap ends with wood screws, making sure the back edges are flush. Set the cap frame on the planter bin so the back edges are flush. Drill pilot holes and counterbore them. Drive 2½" deck screws through the cap frame and into the side and end cleats.

Step 6: Make the Trellis

A. The trellis is made from pieces in a crosshatch pattern. The exact number and placement of the pieces is up to you—use the same spacing we used (see Drawing) or create your own.

B. Cut the end posts (G), center post (H) and rails (I, J, K) to length. Lay the end posts and center post together side by side with their bottom edges flush so you can gang-mark the rail positions.

C. Use a square as a guide for drawing lines across all three posts, 18" up from the bottom. Draw the next line 7½" up from the first. Draw additional lines across the posts, spaced 7½" apart.

D. Cut two 7"-wide scrap blocks and use them to separate the posts as you assemble the trellis. Attach the rails to the posts in the sequence shown in the Diagram, using 2½" screws (photo 4). Alternate from the fronts to the backs of the posts when installing the rails.

Step 7: Apply Finishing Touches

A. Fasten the trellis to the back of the planter bin so the bottoms of the posts rest on the top edge of the base. Drill pilot holes in the posts. Counterbore the holes. Drive 2½" deck screws through the posts and into the cap frame. With a 1"-dia. spade bit, drill a pair of drainage holes in each bottom board. Stain the project with an exterior wood stain.

PLUMBING YOUR GREENHOUSE OR SHED

Flexible polyethylene (PE) pipe is used to extend cold-water plumbing lines to an outdoor fixture, such as a sink located in a shed or detached garage, a lawn sprinkler system, or a garden spigot. In mild climates, outdoor plumbing can remain in service year-round, but in regions with a frost season, the outdoor supply pipes must be drained or blown empty with pressurized air to prevent the pipes from rupturing when the ground freezes.

On the following pages you will see how to run supply pipes from the house to a utility sink in a detached garage. The utility sink drains into a rock-filled dry well installed in the yard. A dry well is designed to handle only "gray water" waste, such as the soapy rinse water created by washing

tools or work clothes. Never use a dry well drain for septic materials, such as animal waste or food scraps. Never pour paints, solvent-based liquids, or solid materials into a sink that drains into a dry well. Such materials will quickly clog up your system and will eventually filter down into the groundwater supply.

Like an indoor sink, the garage utility sink has a vent pipe running up from the drain trap. This vent can extend through the roof, or it can extend through the side wall of the garage and be covered with a screen to keep birds and insects out.

Before digging a trench for an outdoor plumbing line, contact your local utility companies and ask them to mark the locations of underground gas, power, telephone, and water lines.

A single garden spigot and rubber hose will suffice as an irrigation system for small or moderate-sized greenhouses. A watering wand makes this chore easier.

HOW TO Install Outdoor Plumbing for a Utility Sink

1 Plan a convenient route from a ¾" cold-water supply pipe in the basement to the outdoor sink location; then drill a 1"-diameter hole through the sill plate. Drill a similar hole where the pipe will enter the garage. On the ground outside, lay out the pipe run with spray paint or stakes.

2 Use a flat spade to remove sod for an 8"- to 12"-wide trench along the marked route from the house to the garage. Set the sod aside and keep it moist so it can be reused after the project is completed. Dig a trench that slopes slightly (⅛" per foot) toward the house and is at least 10" deep at its shallowest point. Use a long, straight 2 × 4 and a level to ensure that the trench has the correct slope.

3 Below the access hole in the rim joist, dig a small pit and install a plastic valve box so the top is flush with the ground. Lay a thick layer of gravel in the bottom of the box. Dig a similar pit and install a second valve box at the opposite end of the trench, where the water line will enter the garage.

4 Run ¾" PE pipe along the bottom of the trench from the house to the utility sink location. Use insert couplings and stainless steel clamps when it is necessary to join two lengths of pipe.

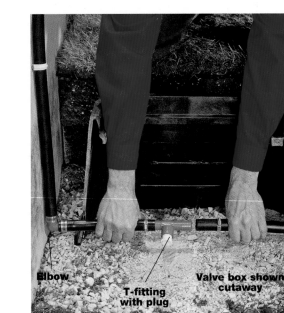

Elbow

T-fitting with plug

Valve box shown cutaway

5 At each end of the trench, extend the pipe through the valve box and up the foundation wall, using a barbed elbow fitting to make the 90° bend. Install a barbed T-fitting with a threaded outlet in the valve box so the threaded portion of the fitting faces down. Insert a male threaded plug in the bottom outlet of the T-fitting.

6 Use barbed elbow fittings to extend the pipe into the basement and garage; then use pipe straps and masonry screws to anchor the PE pipe to the foundation.

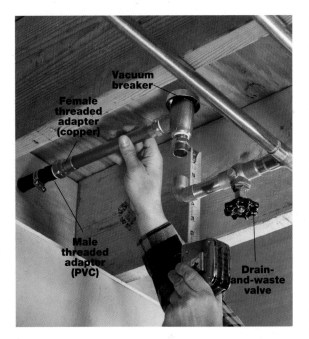

Vacuum breaker

Female threaded adapter (copper)

Male threaded adapter (PVC)

Drain-and-waste valve

7 Inside the house, make the transition between the PE pipe and the copper cold-water supply pipe, using a threaded male PVC adapter, a female threaded copper adapter, a vacuum breaker, a drain-and-waste valve, and a copper T-fitting. The drain-and-waste valve includes a threaded cap, which can be removed to blow water from the lines when you winterize the system.

Sidewalk Crossing

To run pipe under a sidewalk, attach a length of rigid PVC pipe to a garden hose with a pipe-to-hose adapter. Cap the end of the pipe, and drill a ⅛" hole in the center of the cap. Turn on the water, and use the high-pressure stream to bore a tunnel.

8 In the garage, attach a male threaded PVC adapter to the end of the PE pipe; then use a copper female threaded adapter, elbow, and male threaded adapter to extend a copper riser up to a brass hose bib. After completing the supply-pipe installation, fill in the trench, tamping the soil firmly. Install the utility sink, complete with 1½" drain trap and waste T-fitting. Bore a 2" hole in the wall where the sink drain will exit the garage.

9 At least 6 ft. from the garage, dig a pit about 2 ft. in diameter and 3 ft. deep. Punch holes in the sides and bottom of an old trash can, and cut a 2" hole in the side of the can, about 4" from the top edge. Insert the can into the pit; the top edge should be about 6" below ground level. Run 1½" PVC drain pipe from the utility sink to the dry well. Fill the dry well with coarse rock and drape landscape fabric over it; then cover the trench and well with soil and reinstall the sod. Extend a vent pipe up from the waste T through the roof or side wall of the garage.

HOW TO Winterize Outdoor Plumbing Pipes in Cold Climates

Close the drain-and-waste valve for the outdoor supply pipe; then remove the cap on the drain nipple. With the hose bib on the outdoor sink open, attach an air compressor to the valve nipple; then blow water from the system using no more than 50 psi (pounds per square inch) of air pressure. Remove the plugs from the T-fittings in each valve box and store them for the winter.

CONVERSIONS

To Convert:	To:	Multiply by:
Inches	Millimeters	25.4
Inches	Centimeters	2.54
Feet	Meters	0.305
Yards	Meters	0.914
Square inches	Square centimeters	6.45
Square feet	Square meters	0.093
Square yards	Square meters	0.836
Ounces	Milliliters	30.0
Pints (U.S.)	Liters	0.473 (Imp. 0.568)
Quarts (U.S.)	Liters	0.946 (Imp. 1.136)
Gallons (U.S.)	Liters	3.785 (Imp. 4.546)
Ounces	Grams	28.4
Pounds	Kilograms	0.454

To Convert:	To:	Multiply by:
Millimeters	Inches	0.039
Centimeters	Inches	0.394
Meters	Feet	3.28
Meters	Yards	1.09
Square centimeters	Square inches	0.155
Square meters	Square feet	10.8
Square meters	Square yards	1.2
Milliliters	Ounces	.033
Liters	Pints (U.S.)	2.114 (Imp. 1.76)
Liters	Quarts (U.S.)	1.057 (Imp. 0.88)
Liters	Gallons (U.S.)	0.264 (Imp. 0.22)
Grams	Ounces	0.035
Kilograms	Pounds	2.2

Converting Temperatures

Convert degrees Fahrenheit (F) to degrees Celsius (C) by following this simple formula: Subtract 32 from the Fahrenheit temperature reading; then multiply that number by $5/9$. For example, 77°F - 32 = 45. $45 \times 5/9 = 25°C$.

To convert degrees Celsius to degrees Fahrenheit, multiply the Celsius temperature reading by $9/5$; then add 32. For example, $25°C \times 9/5 = 45$. $45 + 32 = 77°F$.

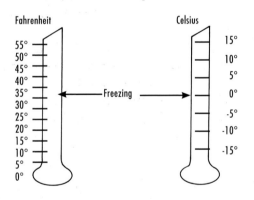

Metric Plywood Panels

Metric plywood panels are commonly available in two sizes: 1,200 mm × 2,400 mm and 1,220 mm × 2,400 mm, which is roughly equivalent to a 4 × 8-ft. sheet. Standard and Select sheathing panels come in standard thicknesses, while Sanded-grade panels are available in special thicknesses.

Standard Sheathing Grade		Sanded Grade	
7.5 mm	(5/16 in.)	6 mm	(4/17 in.)
9.5 mm	(3/8 in.)	8 mm	(5/16 in.)
12.5 mm	(1/2 in.)	11 mm	(7/16 in.)
15.5 mm	(5/8 in.)	14 mm	(9/16 in.)
18.5 mm	(3/4 in.)	17 mm	(2/3 in.)
20.5 mm	(13/16 in.)	19 mm	(3/4 in.)
22.5 mm	(7/8 in.)	21 mm	(13/16 in.)
25.5 mm	(1 in.)	24 mm	(15/16 in.)

Lumber Dimensions

Nominal - U.S.	Actual - U.S. (in inches)	Metric
1 × 2	3/4 × 1½	19 × 38 mm
1 × 3	3/4 × 2½	19 × 64 mm
1 × 4	3/4 × 3½	19 × 89 mm
1 × 5	3/4 × 4½	19 × 114 mm
1 × 6	3/4 × 5½	19 × 140 mm
1 × 7	3/4 × 6¼	19 × 159 mm
1 × 8	3/4 × 7¼	19 × 184 mm
1 × 10	3/4 × 9¼	19 × 235 mm
1 × 12	3/4 × 11¼	19 × 286 mm
1¼ × 4	1 × 3½	25 × 89 mm
1¼ × 6	1 × 5½	25 × 140 mm
1¼ × 8	1 × 7¼	25 × 184 mm
1¼ × 10	1 × 9¼	25 × 235 mm
1¼ × 12	1 × 11¼	25 × 286 mm
1½ × 4	1¼ × 3½	32 × 89 mm
1½ × 6	1¼ × 5½	32 × 140 mm
1½ × 8	1¼ × 7¼	32 × 184 mm
1½ × 10	1¼ × 9¼	32 × 235 mm
1½ × 12	1¼ × 11¼	32 × 286 mm
2 × 4	1½ × 3½	38 × 89 mm
2 × 6	1½ × 5½	38 × 140 mm
2 × 8	1½ × 7¼	38 × 184 mm
2 × 10	1½ × 9¼	38 × 235 mm
2 × 12	1½ × 11¼	38 × 286 mm
3 × 6	2½ × 5½	64 × 140 mm
4 × 4	3½ × 3½	89 × 89 mm
4 × 6	3½ × 5½	89 × 140 mm

Liquid Measurement Equivalents

1 Pint	= 16 Fluid Ounces	= 2 Cups
1 Quart	= 32 Fluid Ounces	= 2 Pints
1 Gallon	= 128 Fluid Ounces	= 4 Quarts

RESOURCES & CREDITS

ACF Greenhouses
888 888 9050
email: help@LittleGreenhouse.com
www.littlegreenhouse.com

Greenhouses.com
800 681 3302
www.greenhouses.com

GreenhouseKit.com
877 718 2865
www.greenhousekit.com

Hoop House Greenhouse Kits
800 760 5192
email: hoop@cape.com
www.househouse.com

Juliana Greenhouses
www.julianagreenhouses.com

North Florida REC (NFREC)
Suwannee Valley
386 362 1725
http://nfrec-sv.ifas.ufl.edu

Sturdi-built Greenhouses
Redwood greenhouse kits
800 334 4115
www.sturdi-built.com

Photography Credits

p. 7 photo © Ann Steer / www.istock.com
p. 45, 46 (lower two), 49 (left) photo courtesy of Sturdi-built
p. 50, 51 photos courtesy of Solar Innovations
p. 52 photo © Robert Weber / www.istock.com
p. 53 photo © Lidian Neeleman / www.istock.com
p. 55 top photo courtesy of Solar Innovations
p. 55 lower photo courtesy of Sturdi-built
p. 57 photo courtesy of Sturdi-built
p. 58 (lower) photo courtesy of Ikea
p. 58 (top) photo courtesy of Sturdi-built
p. 59 all photos courtesy of NFREC; (top right) Robert Hochmuth (Multi County Extension Agent, UF/IFAS North Florida Research and Education Center, Suwannee Valley, Live Oak FL)
p. 69 top photo © Dency Kane
p. 69 lower photo © Jerry Pavia
p. 81 photo © Clive Nichols
p. 87 lower photo courtesy of Summerwood Outdoors, Inc.
p. 88 (inset) photo courtesy of Spirit Elements
p. 89 top photo courtesy of The Betty Mills Company
p. 89 lower photo courtesy of Finley Products, Inc.
p. 97 top left photo courtesy of Greenhouses.com
p. 107 top photos courtesy of NFREC; (larger image) Danielle Treadwell (Organic Specialist, UF/IFAS Horticultural Sciences Dept, Gainesville FL 352-392-1928)
p. 115 lower right photo © Kjell Brynildsen / www.istock.com
p. 115 top photo courtesy of Sturdi-built
p. 152 photo © Annett Vauteck / www.istock.com

INDEX

160

Greenhouses & Garden Sheds